Web Application Development with R Using Shiny

Harness the graphical and statistical power of R and rapidly develop interactive user interfaces using the superb Shiny package

Chris Beeley

[PACKT] open source*
PUBLISHING   community experience distilled

BIRMINGHAM - MUMBAI

Web Application Development with R Using Shiny

First published: October 2013

Production Reference: 1151013

Published by Packt Publishing Ltd.
Livery Place
35 Livery Street
Birmingham B3 2PB, UK.

ISBN 978-1-78328-447-4

www.packtpub.com

Cover Image by Suresh Mogre (suresh.mogre.99@gmail.com)

Credits

Author
Chris Beeley

Reviewers
Neependra Khare
Ram Narasimhan
Hernán G. Resnizky

Acquisition Editor
Kevin Colaco

Commissioning Editor
Shaon Basu

Technical Editors
Aparna Chand
Dennis John

Project Coordinator
Suraj Bist

Proofreader
Joanna McMahon

Indexers
Monica Ajmera Mehta
Tejal R. Soni

Production Coordinator
Prachali Bhiwandkar

Cover Work
Prachali Bhiwandkar

About the Author

Chris Beeley is an Applied Researcher working in healthcare in the UK. He completed his PhD in Psychology at the University of Nottingham in 2009 and now works with Nottinghamshire Healthcare NHS Trust providing statistical analysis and other types of evaluation and reporting using routine data generated within the Trust. Chris has a special interest in the use of regression methods in applied healthcare settings, particularly forensic psychiatric settings, as well as in the collection, analysis, and reporting of patient feedback data.

Chris has been a keen user of R and a passionate advocate of open-source tools within research and healthcare settings since completing his PhD. He has made extensive use of R (and Shiny) to automate analysis and reporting for new patient feedback websites. This was funded by a grant from the NHS Institute for Innovation and made in collaboration with staff, service users, and carers within the Trust, particularly individuals from the Involvement Center.

Acknowledgement

I would like to thank all the staff, service users, and carers at the Involvement Center in Nottinghamshire Healthcare NHS Trust, not only for welcoming me and believing in me but also for making my work meaningful. Helping to better understand and communicate with our service users and carers is the reason why I get out of bed in the morning and work long hours on the website. The book was made much easier with the thought that it might help transform healthcare for everyone's benefit.

I'd like to give a massive thank you to the whole R world, the R core team, the people at RStudio, Joe Cheng, Winston Chang, Hadley Wickham (what was life like before ggplot2?) and all the people I've had so much help from over the years, on mailing lists, forums, blog posts, and wherever else I've found you. Everyone who believes in free and open source believes that by cooperating and sharing we can build a better world, and this is a profound message not just in the world of software, but globally everywhere. I could never hope to give back as much to this community as I've taken already, but I promise to try.

I would also like to thank my wife and son who helped me remember that there's more to life than coding and work, and are, in general, the complete opposite of writing a book about an R package.

About the Reviewers

Neependra Khare has around 9 years of experience in the IT industry. He has worked as a SysAdmin, support engineer, and a filesystem developer. Currently he is working with Red Hat as Principal Software Engineer.

As a data enthusiast, he uses R and Shiny to do the analysis and publish visualizations. More can be found out about him on his website at www.neependra.net.

Ram Narasimhan works in the Data Science group at GE Global Research. He has worked in applied data analysis for over 15 years, including working as a data consultant in multiple verticals (transportation, manufacturing, and supply chain) where his tools of choice were Python and R. He created and managed a data analytics team for United Airlines in Chicago. He has a Master's in Industrial Engineering and a Doctorate in Operations Research.

Hernán G. Resnizky is an experienced Sociologist and Data Analyst with a Masters degree in Data Mining from the University of Buenos Aires. He currently works for Despegar.com, the leading online tourism agency in Latin America, and has previously worked for other top-level companies, such as Microsoft and Ipsos. Currently, Hernán is focused on working with R, covering not only the Data Analysis stage but also Data Extraction, Processing, and Visualization. In his blog, www.hernanresnizky.com (also known as *My Data Atelier*), you can find commented material regarding R and Data Analysis in general.

www.PacktPub.com

Support files, eBooks, discount offers and more

You might want to visit www.PacktPub.com for support files and downloads related to your book.

Did you know that Packt offers eBook versions of every book published, with PDF and ePub files available? You can upgrade to the eBook version at www.PacktPub.com and as a print book customer, you are entitled to a discount on the eBook copy. Get in touch with us at service@packtpub.com for more details.

At www.PacktPub.com, you can also read a collection of free technical articles, sign up for a range of free newsletters and receive exclusive discounts and offers on Packt books and eBooks.

http://PacktLib.PacktPub.com

Do you need instant solutions to your IT questions? PacktLib is Packt's online digital book library. Here, you can access, read and search across Packt's entire library of books.

Why Subscribe?

- Fully searchable across every book published by Packt
- Copy and paste, print and bookmark content
- On demand and accessible via web browser

Free Access for Packt account holders

If you have an account with Packt at www.PacktPub.com, you can use this to access PacktLib today and view nine entirely free books. Simply use your login credentials for immediate access.

I would like to dedicate this book to my dad who always believed in me.
I hope I'm still making him proud.

Table of Contents

Preface

Harness the graphical and statistical power of R, and rapidly develop interactive and engaging user interfaces using the superb Shiny package which makes programming for user interaction simple. R is a highly flexible and powerful tool for analyzing and visualizing data. Shiny is the perfect companion to R, making it quick and simple to share analysis and graphics from R that users can interact with and query over the Web. Let Shiny do the hard work and spend your time generating content and styling, not writing code to handle user inputs. This book is full of practical examples and shows you how to write cutting-edge interactive content for the Web, right from a minimal example all the way to fully styled and extendible applications.

What this book covers

Chapter 1, Installing R and Shiny and Getting Started!, is an introduction to R and Shiny, with advice on using R, picking a code editor, making your first graphics, and a first look at example Shiny applications.

Chapter 2, Building Your First Application, covers the basic structure of a Shiny program, simple widgets and layout functions, and serves as an introduction to reactive programming in Shiny.

Chapter 3, Building Your Own Webpages Pages with Shiny, covers producing custom web content with Shiny, from styling with HTML and CSS to turbo-charging with JavaScript and jQuery.

Chapter 4, Taking Control of Reactivity, Inputs, and Outputs, covers advanced Shiny features, such as showing and hiding elements of the UI, reactive UIs, using client data in your applications, and handling custom data and graphics.

Chapter 5, Running and Sharing Your Creations, shows how to share Shiny applications with fellow R users as well as with the whole world, quickly and simply over the Web.

What you need for this book

All the software discussed in this book is free and open source, and can be downloaded easily for Windows, OS X, and Linux.

Who this book is for

You need no previous experience with R, Shiny, HTML, or CSS to begin using this book, although you will need at least a little previous experience with programming in a different language.

Conventions

In this book, you will find a number of styles of text that distinguish between different kinds of information. Here are some examples of these styles, and an explanation of their meaning.

A block of code is set as follows:

```
output$reacDomains <- renderUI({

  domainList = unique(as.character(passData()$networkDomain))

  selectInput("subDomains", "Choose subdomain", domainList)

})
```

Code words in text are shown as follows: "They should be named server.R and ui.R."

New terms and **important words** are shown in bold. Words that you see on the screen, in menus or dialog boxes for example, appear in the text like this: "You can see the function names (**checkboxGroupInput** and **checkboxInput**) as numbered entries on the left-hand side panel".

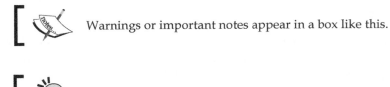

Warnings or important notes appear in a box like this.

Tips and tricks appear like this.

Reader feedback

Feedback from our readers is always welcome. Let us know what you think about this book—what you liked or may have disliked. Reader feedback is important for us to develop titles that you really get the most out of.

To send us general feedback, simply send an e-mail to feedback@packtpub.com, and mention the book title through the subject of your message.

If there is a topic that you have expertise in and you are interested in either writing or contributing to a book, see our author guide on www.packtpub.com/authors.

Customer support

Now that you are the proud owner of a Packt book, we have a number of things to help you to get the most from your purchase.

Downloading the example code

You can download the example code files for all Packt books you have purchased from your account at http://www.packtpub.com. If you purchased this book elsewhere, you can visit http://www.packtpub.com/support and register to have the files e-mailed directly to you.

Errata

Although we have taken every care to ensure the accuracy of our content, mistakes do happen. If you find a mistake in one of our books—maybe a mistake in the text or the code—we would be grateful if you would report this to us. By doing so, you can save other readers from frustration and help us improve subsequent versions of this book. If you find any errata, please report them by visiting http://www.packtpub.com/support, selecting your book, clicking on the **errata submission form** link, and entering the details of your errata. Once your errata are verified, your submission will be accepted and the errata will be uploaded to our website, or added to any list of existing errata, under the Errata section of that title.

Piracy

Piracy of copyright material on the Internet is an ongoing problem across all media. At Packt, we take the protection of our copyright and licenses very seriously. If you come across any illegal copies of our works, in any form, on the Internet, please provide us with the location address or website name immediately so that we can pursue a remedy.

Please contact us at `copyright@packtpub.com` with a link to the suspected pirated material.

We appreciate your help in protecting our authors, and our ability to bring you valuable content.

Questions

You can contact us at `questions@packtpub.com` if you are having a problem with any aspect of the book, and we will do our best to address it.

1
Installing R and Shiny and Getting Started!

If you have heard about R, you probably know that it's free and open source and well on its way to becoming a preeminent tool for statisticians and data scientists. You may be aware that there are over 4000 user-contributed packages available for R, which help users with tasks as diverse as computational chemistry, physics, finance, clinical trials, medical imaging, psychometrics, machine learning, statistical methods, and extremely powerful and flexible statistical graphics.

The Shiny package is a free contributed package to R that makes it incredibly easy to deliver interactive data summaries and queries to end users through any modern web browser. Shiny comes with a variety of widgets for rapidly building user interfaces and does all of the heavy lifting in terms of setting up interactive user interfaces. The default styling of a Shiny application is clean and effective, however Shiny is very extensible and it is easy to integrate Shiny applications with your own web content using HTML and CSS. JavaScript and jQuery can also be used to further extend the scope of Shiny applications.

This book will show you how to build your own web interfaces with Shiny, right from starting with R to integrating them with your own websites. In this chapter, we are going to learn the following:

- Install R, choose an IDE, and have a look at the power and flexibility of R
- Run some examples within R and learn a bit of the R language
- Look at resources to help you learn more about R and Shiny
- Install Shiny, and run and browse the examples

R is a big subject and this is a brief tour. So if you get a little lost along the way, don't worry. This chapter is really all about getting started and helping you recognize some of the languages and data structures you will come across later. You can come back to this chapter once you have got the basics of Shiny and want to start delving a bit deeper; and as you write more and more R code, it will all start to sink in.

Installing R

R is available for Windows, OS X, and Linux at http://cran.r-project.org. The source code is also available at the same address. It is also included in many Linux package management systems. Linux users are advised to check before downloading from the web. Details on installing from source or binary for Windows, OS X, and Linux are all available at http://www.cran.r-project.org/doc/manuals/R-admin.html.

The R console

Windows and OS X users can run the R application to launch the R console. Linux and OS X users can also run the R console straight from the terminal by typing R.

In either case, the R console will look as shown in the following screenshot:

```
R version 3.0.1 (2013-05-16) -- "Good Sport"
Copyright (C) 2013 The R Foundation for Statistical Computing
Platform: x86_64-pc-linux-gnu (64-bit)

R is free software and comes with ABSOLUTELY NO WARRANTY.
You are welcome to redistribute it under certain conditions.
Type 'license()' or 'licence()' for distribution details.

  Natural language support but running in an English locale

R is a collaborative project with many contributors.
Type 'contributors()' for more information and
'citation()' on how to cite R or R packages in publications.

Type 'demo()' for some demos, 'help()' for on-line help, or
'help.start()' for an HTML browser interface to help.
Type 'q()' to quit R.

>
```

R will respond to your commands right from the terminal. Let's have a go:

```
> 2 + 2
[1] 4
```

The [1] tells you that R returned one result, in this case, 4:

```
> print("Hello world!")
[1] "Hello world!"
```

Multiples of pi:

```
> 1:10 * pi
[1]    3.141593   6.283185   9.424778 12.566371 15.707963 18.849556
[7] 21.991149 25.132741 28.274334 31.415927
```

This example illustrates vector-based programming in R. 1:10 generates the numbers 1 to 10 as a vector, and each is then multiplied by pi, returning another vector, the elements each being pi times larger than the original. Operating on vectors is an important part of writing simple and efficient R code. As you can see, R again numbers the values it returns at the console, with the seventh value being 21.99.

Before we leave the console, let's have a quick look at some of the graphics capability within R:

```
> demo(graphics)
```

Or:

```
> demo(persp)
```

Code editors and IDEs

The Windows and OS X versions of R both come with built-in code editors which allow code to be edited, saved, and sent to the R console. Choice of code editors and IDEs is a highly personal decision and if you are just starting out with R, you would best be advised to try a few before settling on one. Following are some choices in this area, available for all the three platforms except where specified otherwise.

Simple and well-featured

These are ideal for beginners:

- **Notepad ++ with the NppToR plugin** (Windows only): This supports code highlighting, execution of blocks of code, and a few other useful features
- **RKWard**: This includes data editing, data import, and package management

- **Tinn-R** (Windows only): This supports some other languages as well as LaTeX, and includes project management functions
- **RStudio**: It is very well-featured (and my personal favorite), with project management and version control (including support for Git), viewing of data and graphics, code-completion, package management, and many other features

Complex and extensible

These are ideal for those who are already using other text editors and IDEs. The following plugins are available for R:

- **Emacs with the Emacs Speaks Statistics plugin**: Emacs is favored by many for its level of extensibility and support for, well, everything (programming languages, markup languages, project management, e-mail, and even web browsing)
- **Vim with the Vim-R plugin**: Like Emacs, Vim is a highly extensible package which supports many programming and markup languages and is extremely powerful
- **Eclipse with the StatET plugin**: It is a very well-featured and extensible IDE for R, Java, HTML, and many others

Learning R

There are almost as many uses of R as there are people using it. It is not possible to cover all your specific needs within this book. However, it is likely that you may wish to use R to process, query, and visualize data, such as sales figures, satisfaction surveys, concurrent users, sporting results, or whatever type of data your organization processes. The next chapters will concentrate on Google Analytics data downloaded from the **Application Programming Interface (API)**, but for now, let's just have a look at the basics.

Getting help

There are many books and online materials covering all the aspects of R. The name R can make it difficult to come up with useful web-search hits (substituting CRAN for R can sometimes help); nonetheless, searching for *R tutorial* does give useful results. Some useful resources include the following:

An excellent introduction to the syntax and data structures in R can be found at
`http://goo.gl/M0RQ5z`.

You can watch videos on using R from Google at `http://goo.gl/A3uRsh`.

Quick-R provides a lot of useful code and examples that can be found at `http://www.statmethods.net/`.

At the R console, typing `?` followed by the function name (for example, `?help`) brings up help materials, and the command `??help` will bring up a list of potentially relevant functions from the installed packages.

Subscribing to and asking questions on the R-help mailing list at `http://www.r-project.org/mail.html` allows you to communicate with some of the leading figures in the R community as well as many other talented enthusiasts. Do read the posting guide and research your question before you ask any questions because contributors to the list are often busy and can be unforgiving of poor questions.

There are two Stack Exchange communities which can provide further help that can be accessed at `http://stats.stackexchange.com/` (for questions on statistics and visualization with R) and `http://stackoverflow.com/` (for questions on programming with R).

Loading data

The simplest way to load data into R is probably using a comma separated value (`.csv`) spreadsheet file, which can be downloaded from many data sources, and loaded and saved in all spreadsheet software (such as Excel or LibreOffice). The `read.table()` command imports data of this type by specifying the separator as a comma, or there is a function specifically for `.csv` files, `read.csv()`:

```
> analyticsData <-
    read.table("C:\\Mydocuments\\Data\\Analytics.csv",
    sep = ",")
```

Or:

```
> analyticsData <-
    read.csv("C:\\Mydocuments\\Data\\Analytics.csv")
```

Note that unlike in other languages, R uses `<-` as well as `=` for assignment. Assignment can be made the other way using `->`. The result of this is that y can be told to hold the value of 4 in this way `y <- 4` or like this `4 -> y`. There are some other, more advanced, things that can be done with assignment in R, but don't worry about them now. Just write code using the assignment operator as shown in the previous example and you'll be just like the natives that you come across on forums and blog posts.

Either of the previous code examples will assign the contents of the `Analytics.csv` file to a dataframe called `analyticsData`, with the first row of the spreadsheet providing the variable names. A dataframe is a special type of object in R which is designed to be useful for the storage and analysis of data.

Dataframes, lists, arrays, and matrices

Dataframes have several important features which make them useful for data analysis:

- Rectangular data structures: In general, the pieces of data will read down the rows (for example, consecutive dates in June) and each variable (for example, unique visitors or time spent on the site) for these cases will read across the columns. A mix of datatypes is supported. A typical dataframe might include variables containing dates, numbers (integer or float), and text.

- Subsetting and variable extraction can be easily done. R provides a lot of built-in functionality to select rows and variables within a dataframe.

- Many functions include a data argument which makes it very simple to pass dataframes to functions, and process only those variables and cases that are relevant, which makes for cleaner and simpler code

We can inspect the first few rows of the dataframe using the `head(analyticsData)` command as shown in the following screenshot:

```
> head(analyticsData)
         Day pageViews uniqueVisitors visitDuration
1 2013-06-01       572             21      7.843611
2 2013-06-02       955             36      8.555000
3 2013-06-03       993             48     17.959722
4 2013-06-04       553             41     20.997500
5 2013-06-05       654             16     12.221111
6 2013-06-06       878             47      8.250278
>
```

As you can see, there are four variables within the dataframe: one contains dates, two are integer variables, and the last is a numeric variable. There is more about variable types in R following.

Variables can be extracted from dataframes simply using the `$` operator:

```
> analyticsData$pageViews
 [1] 836 676 940 689 647 899 934 718 776 570 651 816
[13] 731 604 627 946 634 990 994 599 657 642 894 983
[25] 646 540 756 989 965 821
```

Or using `[]`:

```
> analyticsData[, "pageViews"]
```

Note the use of the comma with nothing before it to indicate that all the rows are required. If a subset of rows were required, it could be achieved through the following command line:

```
> analyticsData[1:10,"pageViews"]
[1] 836 676 940 689 647 899 934 718 776 570
```

In the same way, leaving a blank space after the comma returns all the variables:

```
> analyticsData[1:3,]
```

```
> analyticsData[1:3,]
        Day pageViews uniqueVisitors visitDuration
1 2013-06-01       572             21      7.843611
2 2013-06-02       955             36      8.555000
3 2013-06-03       993             48     17.959722
>
```

Dataframes are a special type of list. Lists can hold many different types of data, including lists. As with many datatypes in R, their elements can be named, which can be very useful for writing code that is easy to understand. Let's make a list of the options for dinner, with drink quantities expressed in milliliters.

In the following example, please note the use of the `c()` function which is used to produce vectors and lists by giving their elements separated by commas. R will pick an appropriate class for the return value: string for vectors that contain strings, numeric for those that only contain numbers, logical for boolean values, and so on:

```
> dinnerList <- list("Vegetables" =
    c("Potatoes", "Cabbage", "Carrots"),
    "Dessert" = c("Ice cream", "Apple pie"),
    "Drinks" = c(250, 330, 500)
    )
```

Indexing is similar to that of dataframes (which are, after all, special instances of a list). They can be indexed by number as shown in the following command lines:

```
> dinnerList[1:2]
$Vegetables
[1] "Potatoes" "Cabbage"  "Carrots"
```

```
$Dessert
[1] "Ice cream" "Apple pie"
```

This returns a list. Returning an object of the appropriate class is achieved using `[[]]`:

```
> dinnerList[[3]]
[1] 250 330 500
```

In this case, a numeric vector is returned. They can be indexed by name also:

```
> dinnerList["Drinks"]
$Drinks
[1] 250 330 500
```

Note that this also returns a list.

Matrices and arrays, unlike dataframes, only hold one type of data and make use of square brackets for indexing. Thus, the command `analyticsMatrix[, 3:6]` returns all the rows from the third to the sixth column; `analyticsMatrix[1, 3]` returns just the first row of the third column; and `analyticsArray[1, 2, ]` returns the first row of the second column across all the elements within the third dimension.

Variable types

R is a dynamically typed language and so you are not required to declare the type of your variables. It is worth knowing, of course, about the different types of variables that you might read or write using R. The different types of variables can be stored in a variety of structures, such as vectors, matrices, and dataframes, although some restrictions apply as detailed previously (for example, matrices must contain only one variable type). Declaring a variable with at least one string will produce a vector of strings (in R, the character datatype):

```
> c("First", "Third", 4, "Second")
[1] "First"  "Third"  "4"      "Second"
```

Declaring a variable with just numbers will produce a numeric vector:

```
> c(15, 10, 20, 11, 0.4, -4)
[1] 15.0 10.0 20.0 11.0  0.4 -4.0
```

R includes a logical datatype also:

```
> c(TRUE, FALSE, TRUE, TRUE, FALSE)
[1]  TRUE FALSE  TRUE  TRUE FALSE
```

A datatype exists for dates as well and is often a problem for beginners:

```
> as.Date(c("2013/10/24", "2012/12/05", "2011/09/02"))
[1] "2013-10-24" "2012-12-05" "2011-09-02"
```

The use of the `factor` datatype tells R of all the possible values of a categorical variable, such as gender or species:

```
> factor(c("Male", "Female", "Female", "Male", "Male"),
                  levels = c("Female", "Male")
[1] Male    Female Female Male    Male
Levels: Female Male
```

Functions

As you grow in confidence with R, you will wish to begin writing your own functions. This is achieved very simply and in a manner quite reminiscent of many other languages. You will undoubtedly wish to read more about writing functions in R in a fuller treatment, but just to give you an idea, here is a function called `sumMultiply` which adds together x and y and multiplies that value by z:

```
sumMultiply <- function(x, y, z){
  final = (x+y) * z
  return(final)
}
```

Objects

There are many special object types within R designed to make it easier to analyze data. Functions in R can be polymorphic, that is, they can respond to different datatypes in different ways in order to produce the output that the user desires. For example, the `plot()` function in R responds to a wide variety of datatypes and objects, including single dimension vectors (each value of y plotted sequentially) and two dimensional matrices (producing a scatterplot), as well as specialized statistical objects such as regression models and time series data. In the latter case, plots specialized for these purposes are produced.

As with the rest of this introduction, don't worry if you haven't written functions before, or don't understand object concepts and aren't sure what all this means. You can produce great applications without understanding all these things, but as you work more and more with R, you will start wanting to learn in more detail about how R works and how experts produce R code. This introduction is designed to give you a jumping-off point to learn more about how to get the best out of R (and Shiny).

Base graphics and ggplot2

There are a lot of user-contributed graphics packages in R that can produce some wonderful graphics. You may wish to have a look for yourself at the CRAN task view that can be found at `http://cran.r-project.org/web/views/Graphics.html`. We will have a very quick look at two approaches: base graphics, so called because it is the default graphical environment within a vanilla install of R; and ggplot2, a highly popular user-contributed package produced by Hadley Wickham which is a little trickier to master than base graphics but can rapidly produce a wide range of graphical data summaries. We will cover two graphs familiar to all: the bar chart and the line chart.

Bar chart

Useful when comparing quantities across categories, bar charts are very simple to use in base graphics, particularly when combined with the `table()` command. We will use the mpg dataset which comes with the ggplot2 package; it summarizes different characteristics of a range of cars. First, let's install the ggplot2 package. You can do this straight from the console:

```
> install.packages("ggplot2")
```

You can also use the built-in package functions in IDEs, such as RStudio or RKWard. We will need to load the package every time we wish to use this dataset or the ggplot2 package itself. We need to give the following command at the console:

```
> library(ggplot2)
```

We will use the `table()` command to count the number of each type of car featured in the dataset:

```
> table(mpg$class)
```

This returns a table object (another special object type within R) that contains a frequency count for each type of car as seen in the following screenshot:

```
> table(mpg$class)

 2seater   compact   midsize   minivan    pickup subcompact       suv
       5        47        41        11        33        35        62
>
```

Producing a bar chart of this object is achieved through the following command line:

```
> barplot(table(mpg$class), main = "Base graphics")
```

The `barplot( )` function takes a vector of frequencies. When they are named, as in the previous example (the `table()` command returns the named frequencies in the table form), the names are automatically included on the x-axis. The defaults for this graph are rather plain. Explore `?barplot` and `?par` to learn more about fine-tuning your graphics.

We have already loaded the ggplot2 package in order to use the mpg dataset, but if you have shut down R in between these two examples, you will need to reload it by the following command line:

```
> library(ggplot2)
```

The same graph is produced in ggplot2 in the following way:

```
> ggplot(data = mpg, aes(x = class)) + geom_bar() +

    ggtitle("ggplot2")
```

This `ggplot` call shows the three fundamental elements of ggplot calls: the use of a dataframe (`data = mpg`), the setting up of aesthetics (`aes(x = class)`) which determines how variables are mapped onto axes, colors, and other visual features; and the use of `+ geom_xxx()`. A `ggplot` call sets up the data and aesthetics, but does not plot anything. Functions such as `geom_bar()` (there are many others, see `??geom`) tell ggplot what type of a graph to plot, as well as taking optional arguments, for example, `geom_bar()` optionally takes a position argument which defines whether the bars should be stacked, offset, or stretched to a common height to show proportions instead of frequencies.

These elements are the key to the power and flexibility that ggplot2 offers. Once the data structure is defined, ways of visualizing it can be added and taken away easily, not only in terms of the type of graphic (bar, line, scatter) but also the scales and co-ordinate system (log10, polar co-ordinates), and statistical transformations (smoothing data, summarizing over spatial co-ordinates). The appearance of plots can be easily changed with pre-set and user-defined themes, and multiple plots can be added in layers (that is, adding to one plot) or facets (that is, drawing multiple plots with one function call).

Line chart

Line charts are most often used to indicate change, particularly over a period of time. This time we will use the `longley` dataset, featuring economic variables between 1947 and 1962:

```
> plot(x = 1947 : 1962, y = longley$GNP, type = "l",
        xlab = "Year", main = "Base graphics")
```

The x axis is given by `1947 : 1962`, which enumerates all the numbers between 1947 and 1962, and the `type = "l"` argument specifies the plotting of lines. For other graphs, you may prefer to specify p for just drawing each individual datapoint, or b for drawing both datapoints and lines.

The `ggplot` call looks a lot like it did in the case of the bar chart except with an x and y dimension in the aesthetics this time:

```
> ggplot(longley, aes(x = 1947 : 1962, y = GNP)) + geom_line() +
        xlab("Year") + ggtitle("ggplot2")
```

Base graphics and ggplot versions of the bar chart are shown in the following screenshot for the purpose of comparison:

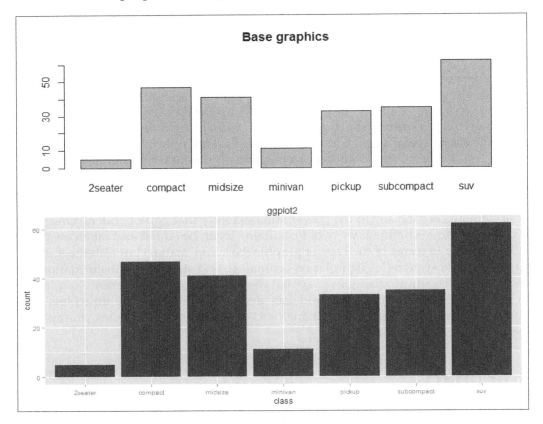

Installing Shiny and running the examples

RKWard, RStudio, and other GUIs include package management functions which can be used to install Shiny, or else it can be very easily installed by typing `install.packages("shiny")` at the console.

Let's run some of the examples:

```
> library(shiny)
```

```
> runExample("01_hello")
```

Your web browser should launch and display the following:

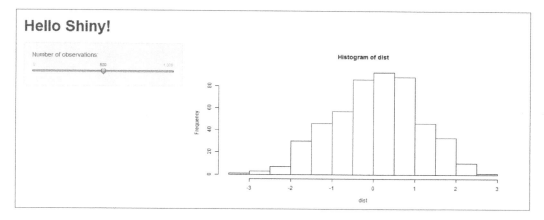

The previous graph shows the frequency of a set of random numbers drawn from a statistical distribution known as the normal distribution, and the slider allows users to select the size of the draw from 0 to 1000. You will notice that when you move the slider, the graph gets updated automatically. This is a fundamental feature of Shiny, which makes use of a **reactive programming paradigm**. Put simply, this is a type of programming which uses reactive expressions that keep track of the values on which they are based that can change (known as reactive values) and update themselves whenever any of their reactive values change. So, in this example, the function that generates the random data and draws the graph is a reactive expression, and the number of random draws which it makes is a reactive value on which the expression depends. Thus whenever the number of draws changes, the function re-executes.

You can find more information on this example, as well as a comprehensive tutorial for Shiny at `http://rstudio.github.io/shiny/tutorial/`.

Notice the layout and style of the web page. Shiny is based on the twitter bootstrap theme by default. However, you are not limited by the styling at all and can build the whole UI using a mix of HTML, CSS, and Shiny code.

Let's look at an interface made with bare-bones HTML and Shiny. Note that in this and all the subsequent examples, we're going to assume that you run `library(shiny)` at the beginning of each session. You don't have to run it before each example but just at the beginning of each R session. So, if you have closed R and come back, do run it at the console. If you can't remember whether you have already done so, run it again to be sure; it won't do any harm:

```
> runExample("08_html")
```

And here it is in all its customizable glory:

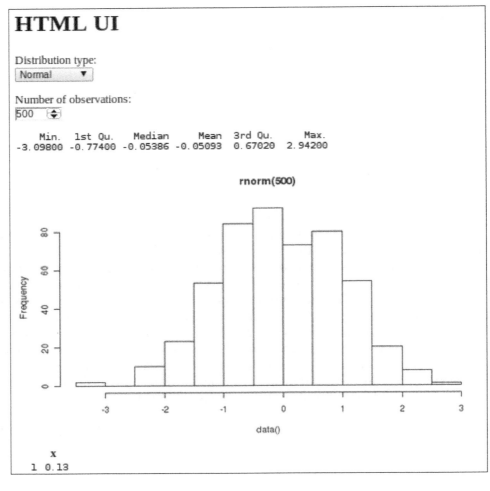

This time there are a few different statistical distributions to pick from, and a different method for selecting the number of observations. By now, you should be looking at the web page and imagining all the possibilities that exist to produce your own interactive data summaries and styling them just how you want, quickly and simply. By the end of the next chapter, you will have made your own application with the default UI, and by the end of the book, you will have gained complete control over the styling and be pondering about where else you can go.

There are a lot of other examples included within the Shiny library. Just type `runExample()` at the console to be provided with the list.

To see some really powerful and well-featured Shiny applications, have a look at the showcase available at `http://www.rstudio.com/shiny/showcase/`.

Summary

In this chapter, we learned how to install R and explored the different options for GUIs and IDEs, and looked at some examples of the graphical power of R. We also learned a little about the data structures of R and looked at some basic visualization code. Finally, we installed Shiny, ran the examples included in the package, and got introduced to a couple of basic concepts within Shiny.

In the next chapter, we will go on to build our own Shiny application using the default UI.

2

Building Your First Application

In the previous chapter we've looked at R, learned some of its basic syntax, and seen some examples of the power and flexibility that R and Shiny offer. This chapter introduces the basics of Shiny. In this chapter we're going to build our own application to interactively query results from the Google Analytics API. We will cover the following topics:

- Basic structure of a Shiny program
- Selection of simple input widgets (checkboxes and radio buttons)
- Selection of simple output types (rendering plots and returning text)
- Selection of simple layout types (page with sidebar and tabbed output panel)
- Handling reactivity in Shiny

Program structure

In this chapter, in just a few pages, we're going to go from the absolute basics of building a program to interactively query data downloaded from the Google Analytics API. Let's get started by having a look at a minimal example of a Shiny program. The first thing to note is that Shiny programs are the easiest to build and understand using two scripts, which are kept within the same folder. They should be named server.R and ui.R. Throughout this book, all code will have a commented server.R and ui.R header to indicate which code goes in which file.

ui.R of minimal example

The ui.R file is a description of the UI and is often the shortest and simplest part of a Shiny application. Note the use of the # character, which marks lines of code as comments that will not be run, but which are for the benefit of humans producing the code:

```
####################################
##### minimal example - ui.R  #####
####################################

library(shiny) # load shiny at beginning at both scripts

shinyUI(pageWithSidebar( # standard shiny layout, controls on the
                                    # left, output on the right

  headerPanel("Minimal example"), # give the interface a title
  sidebarPanel( # all the UI controls go in here

    textInput(inputId = "comment",   # this is the name of the
                               # variable- this will be
                               # passed to server.R

             label = "Say something?", # display label for the
                                    # variable

             value = "" # initial value
    )
  ),

  mainPanel( # all of the output elements go in here
    h3("This is you saying it"), # title with HTML helper
    textOutput("textDisplay")  # this is the name of the output
                          # element as defined in server.R
  )
))
```

To run a Shiny program on your local machine you just need to do the following:

1. Make sure that server.R and ui.R are in the same folder.
2. Make this the R's working directory (using the setwd() command, for example setwd("~/shinyFiles/minimalExample")).
3. Load the Shiny package (library(shiny)).
4. Type runApp() at the console.

runApp() with the name of a directory within works just as well, for example, runApp("~/shinyFiles/minimalExample"). Just remember that it is a directory and not a file that you need to point to.

Let's have a detailed look at the file. We open by loading the Shiny package. You should always do that in both server.R and ui.R files. The first instruction, shinyUI(pageWithSidebar(... tells Shiny that we are using the vanilla UI layout, which places all the controls on the left-hand side and gives you a large space on the right-hand side to include graphs, tables, and text. All of the UI elements are defined within this instruction.

The next line, headerPanel(), gives the application a title. The next two instructions perform the main UI setup, with sidebarPanel() setting up the application controls and mainPanel() setting up the output area. sidebarPanel() will usually contain all of the input widgets, in this case there is only one: textInput(). textInput() is a simple widget that collects text from a textbox that users can interact with using the keyboard. The arguments are pretty typical among most of the widgets and are as follows:

- inputId: This argument names the variable so it can be referred to in the server.R file

- label: This argument gives a label to attach to the input so users know what it does

- value: This argument gives the initial value to the widget when it is set up—all the widgets have sensible defaults for this argument, in this case, it is a blank string, ""

When you are starting out, it can be a good idea to spell out the default arguments in your code until you get used to which function contains which arguments. It also makes your code more readable and reminds you what the return value of the function is (for example, value = TRUE would suggest a Boolean return).

The final function is mainPanel(), which sets up the output window. You can see I have used one of the HTML helper functions to make a little title h3("..."). There are several of these functions designed to generate HTML to go straight on the page; type ?p at the console for the complete list. The other element that goes in mainPanel() is an area for handling reactive text generated within the server.R file—that is, a call to textOutput() with the name of the output as defined in server.R, in this case, "textDisplay".

The finished interface looks similar to the following screenshot:

If you're getting a little bit lost, don't worry. Basically Shiny is just setting up a framework of named input and output elements; the input elements are defined in ui.R and processed by server.R, which then sends them back to ui.R that knows where they all go and what types of output they are.

server.R of minimal example

Let's look now at server.R where it should all become clear:

```
######################################
##### minimal example - server.R #####
######################################

library(shiny) # load shiny at beginning at both scripts

shinyServer(function(input, output) { # server is defined within
                                      # these parentheses

  output$textDisplay <- renderText({ # mark function as reactive
                                     # and assign to
                                     # output$textDisplay for
                                     # passing to ui.R

    paste0("You said '", input$comment,          # from the text
           "'. There are ", nchar(input$comment), # input control as
" characters in this."                           # defined in ui.R
    )
  })
})
```

Let's go through line by line again. We can see again that the package is loaded first using `library(shiny)`. Note that any data read instructions or data processing that just needs to be done once, will also go in this first section (we'll see more about this as we go through the book). `shinyServer(...{...})` defines the bit of Shiny that's going to handle all the data. On the whole, two types of things go in here. Reactive objects (for example, data) are defined, which are then passed around as needed (for example, to different output instructions), and outputs are defined, such as graphs. This simple example contains only the latter. We'll see an example of the first type in the next example.

An output element is defined next with `output$textDsiplay <- renderText({..})`. This instruction does two basic things: firstly, it gives the output a name (`textDisplay`) so it can be referenced in `ui.R` (you can see it in the last part of `ui.R`). Secondly, it tells Shiny that the content contained within is reactive (that is, to be updated when its inputs changes) and that it takes the form of text. We cover advanced concepts in reactive programming with Shiny in a later chapter. There are many excellent illustrations of reactive programming at the Shiny tutorial pages `http://rstudio.github.io/shiny/tutorial/#reactivity-overview`.

The actual processing is very simple in this example. Inputs are read from `ui.R` by the use of `input$...`, so the element named in `ui.R` as `comment` (go and have a look at `ui.R` now to find it) is referenced with `input$comment`.

The whole command uses `paste0()` to link strings with no spaces (equivalent to `paste(..., sep = "")`), picks up the text the user inputted with `input$comment`, and prints it along with the number of characters within it (`nchar()`) and some explanatory text.

That's it! Your first Shiny application is ready. Using these very simple building blocks you can actually make some really useful and engaging applications.

Optional exercise

If you want to have a practice before we move on, take the existing code and modify it so that the output is a plot of a user-defined number of observations, with the text as the title of the plot. The plot call should look like the following:

```
hist(rnorm(XXXX), main = "YYYY")
```

In the preceding line of code XXXX is a number taken from a function in `ui.R` that you will add (`sliderInput()` or `numericInput()`) and YYYY is the text output we already used in the minimal example. You will also need to make use of `renderPlot()`, type `?renderPlot` in the console for more details.

So far in this chapter we have looked at a minimal example, learned about the basic commands that go in the server.R and ui.R files. Thinking about what we've done in terms of reactivity, the ui.R file defines a reactive value, input$comment. The server.R file defines a reactive expression, renderText(), that depends on input$comment. Note that this dependence is defined automatically by Shiny. renderText() uses an output from input$comment, so Shiny automatically connects them. Whenever input$comment changes, renderText() will automatically run with the new value. The extra credit exercise gave two reactive values to the renderPlot() call, and so, whenever either changes, renderPlot() will rerun. In the rest of this chapter we will look at an application that uses some slightly more advanced reactivity concepts, and by the end of the book, we will have covered all the possibilities that Shiny offers and when to use them.

Widget types

Before we move on to a more advanced application, let's have a look at the main widgets that you will make use of within Shiny. I've built a Shiny application that will show you what they all look like, as well as showing their outputs and the type of data they return. To run it, just enter the following command:

```
> runGist(6571951)
```

This is one of several built-in functions of Shiny that allow you to run code hosted on the Internet. Details about sharing your own creations and other ways are discussed in *Chapter 5, Running and Sharing Your Creations*. The finished application looks like the following:

Widget values and data types

1. checkboxGroupInput
   - ☑ Ice cream
   - ☑ Trifle
   - ☐ Pistachios

☑ 2. checkboxInput

3. dateInput

2013-09-15

4. dateRangeInput

2013-08-25	to	2013-09-27

5. numericInput

6	▲▼

6. radioButtons
   - ⊙ Taxi
   - ⦿ Take a walk

7. selectInput

Situation comedy ▾

8. sliderInput

1 ———————————————7————————— 10

9. textInput

Hello, world!

Output and data type

	Value	Class
1	IC,Trifle	character
2	TRUE	logical
3	2013-09-15	Date
4	2013-08-25 2013-09-27	Date
5	6	numeric
6	Walk	character
7	Sitcom	character
8	7	numeric
9	Hello, world!	character

You can see the function names (**checkboxGroupInput** and **checkboxInput**) as numbered entries on the left-hand side panel; for more details, just type `?checkboxGroupInput` at the console.

If you're curious about the code, it's available at `https://gist.github.com/ChrisBeeley/6571951`.

Google Analytics application

Now that we've got the basics, let's build something useful. We're going to build an application that allows you to interactively query data from the Google Analytics API. There is no room within this book to discuss registering for and using the Google Analytics API; however, you will very likely wish to make use of the wonderful **rga** package if you want to get your own Analytics data into R. This package provides an interface between the API and R; at the time of writing, it is still in development and cannot be downloaded using standard package management. Instructions for downloading, installing, and using rga can be found at `https://github.com/skardhamar/rga`.

To keep things simple, we will concentrate on data from a website that I worked on. We'll also use a saved copy of the data that is loaded into the application the first time it runs. A full production of the application could obviously query the API every time it launched or on a daily or weekly basis, depending on how many users you expected (the API limits the number of daily queries from each application). Note that we would *not* query the API as part of a reactive expression unless there was a clear need for the application to be constantly up-to-date, because it would use a lot of the allocated queries, as well as making the program run a lot more slowly. In practice, this means the query, just like the data load function used in the following code, would be given at the top of the `server.R` file, outside of the call to `shinyServer({...})`. It will be launched each time the application is run (or it is trivially simple to write code that ensures this only occurs once per day with the results stored until the application is launched on the next day).

If you like any of the analysis that we come up with or want to extend it, you can always import your own Analytics data and load it in, as here, or query the API online if you want the application to be simple for others to use. All the data and code is hosted on GitHub and can be downloaded from `http://github.com/ChrisBeeley/GoogleAnalytics`.

The UI

If you can, download and run the code and data (the data goes in the same folder as the code) so you can get an idea of what everything does. If you want to run the program without copying the actual data and code to your computer (copying data and code is preferable, so you can play with it), just use another function for sharing and running applications (we will discuss this in *Chapter 5, Running and Sharing Your Creations*):

```
> runGitHub("GoogleAnalytics", "ChrisBeeley")
```

In simple terms, the program allows you to select a date and time range and then view a text summary, or a plot of monthly or hourly figures. There are three tabbed windows in the output region where users can select the type of output they want (**Summary**, **Monthly figures**, and **Hourly figures**).

The data is from a health service (known locally as NHS) website, so users might be interested to show data that originates from domains within the NHS and compare it with data that originates from all other domains. There is an option to add a smoothed line to the graph, and three types of data are available: number of unique visitors, bounce rate (how many users leave the site after the first page they land on), and the average amount of time users spend on the site.

The following screenshot shows it in action:

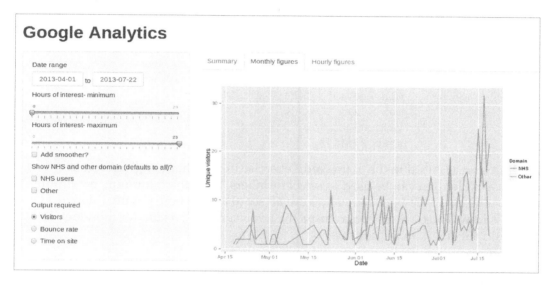

As in many Shiny applications, ui.R is by far the simpler of the two code files and is as follows:

```
###################################
##### Google Analytics - ui.R #####
###################################

library(shiny)

shinyUI(pageWithSidebar(

  headerPanel("Google Analytics"),
```

```
sidebarPanel(

    dateRangeInput(inputId = "dateRange",
                   label = "Date range",
                   start = "2013-04-01",
                   max = Sys.Date()
    ),
```

`dateRangeInput()` gives you two nice date widgets for the user to select a start and end point. As you can see, it's given a name and a label as usual; you can specify the start and end date (as done here, don't use the default behavior which gives the current system date) as well as a maximum date (manually given `Sys.Date()`, that is the system date, as used in this case). There are a lot of other ways to customize, such as the way the date is displayed in the browser, whether the view defaults to months, years, or decades, and others. Type `?dateRangeInput` in the console for more information:

```
sliderInput(inputId = "minimumTime",
            label = "Hours of interest- minimum",
            min = 0,
            max = 23,
            value = 0,
            step = 1),
```

`sliderInput()`, used in the extra credit exercise in this chapter, gives you a graphical slider that can be used to select numbers. Here the minimum, maximum, initial value, and step between values are all set (0 and 23 hours, with a step of 1, which is how Google Analytics returns the `hour` variable); again, for more details type `?sliderInput` in the console:

```
sliderInput(inputId = "maximumTime",
            label = "Hours of interest- maximum",
            min = 0,
            max = 23,
            value = 23,
            step = 1),

checkboxInput(inputId = "smoother",
              label = "Add smoother?",
              value = FALSE),
```

`checkboxInput()` very simply gives you a tick box that returns TRUE when ticked and FALSE when unticked. This example includes all the possible arguments, giving it a name and label and selecting the initial value:

```
checkboxGroupInput(inputId = "domainShow",
                   label = "Show NHS and other domain
                            (defaults to all)?",
                   choices = list("NHS users" = "NHS",
                                  "Other" = "Other")
                   ),
```

`checkboxGroupInput()` returns several checkboxes and is useful when users need to make multiple selections. Of note in this example is the use of a list to specify the options. This allows the display value (given to the user on the UI) and the return value (given to R for processing) to be different. Note the way elements in a list are named; it's quite a simple syntax: `list("First name" = "returnValue1", "Second name" = "returnValue2")`. You can see that this allows nicely formatted labels (with spaces in natural English) to be used in the label and computer-speak (camel case variable names with no spaces) to be used in the return value:

```
radioButtons(inputId = "outputType",
             label = "Output required",
             choices = list("Visitors" = "visitors",
                            "Bounce rate" = "bounceRate",
                            "Time on site" = "timeOnSite"))
```

`radioButtons()`, amazingly, will give you radio buttons. This allows the selection of one thing and one thing only from a list. Again, because a named list is used, an optional `(...selected = ...)` argument can be used to determine the default selection, otherwise the first value is used as the default:

```
      ),
      mainPanel(
        tabsetPanel(
          tabPanel("Summary", textOutput("textDisplay")),
          tabPanel("Monthly figures", plotOutput("monthGraph")),
          tabPanel("Hourly figures", plotOutput("hourGraph"))
        )
      )
))
```

Probably the most unfamiliar part of this code is the use of `tabsetPanel()`. This allows multiple frames of output to be shown on the screen and selected by the user, as is common in GUIs that support tabbed frames. Note that processing is only carried out for the currently selected tab; invisible tabs are not updated behind the scenes but rather when they are made active. This is useful to know where some or all tabs require significant data processing.

The setup is very simple, with a call to `tabsetPanel()` containing several calls to `tabPanel()` in which each of the tabs is defined with a heading and a piece of output, as defined in `server.R`.

Data processing

As you write more and more complex programs, it's the `server.R` file that will become the largest because this is where all the data processing and output goes on, and even where some of the functions that handle advanced UI features live. Instead of going through all of the code line by line, as we did before, we're going to look at the chunks in order and talk about the kinds of things that are done in each section in typical Shiny applications.

The first chunk of code looks like the following:

```
#######################################
#### Google Analytics - server.R #####
#######################################

library(shiny)
library(plyr)
library(ggplot2)

load("analytics.Rdata") # load the dataframe
```

This chunk is run once every time the application is launched. This is where all the data preparation will take place. In this example, it is very simple, and once the relevant R packages are loaded, the whole dataframe is loaded in ready for use. Sometimes you will be able to do all of your data processing "offline" and load the data in, being fully prepared in this way. Sometimes, however, you may rely on a spreadsheet that changes on the server regularly, or, as in this case, you may wish to query the Google API. In cases like these, this is the place to do the data cleaning and preparation necessary to run the R code with the dataset. The code to do that is outside the scope of this section, but it suffices to say that as you get more confident with R, you will be analyzing more and more complex datasets and you will find it useful to do more data preparation within this section.

Reactive objects

The next section is contained within the reactive part contained within the
shinyServer({...}) call. Up until now this section has just contained a list of
output commands that produce the output ready to fill the allocated spaces in ui.R.
In the next chunk we're going to look at another way of managing your analysis.
Sometimes you want to prepare a reactive dataset once and then pass it around the
program as needed. This might be because you have tabbed output windows (as in
this case) that use the same dataset and you don't want to write and maintain code
that prepares the data according to the values of reactive inputs within all three
functions. There are other times when you want to control the processing of data
because it is time-intensive or it might make an online query (such as in the case of
a "live" Google Analytics application that queries data live in response to reactive
inputs). The way that you can take more control over data processing from reactive
inputs, rather than distributing it through your output code, is to use reactive objects.
A **reactive object**, like a reactive function, changes when its input changes. Unlike a
reactive function, it doesn't do anything, but is just a data object (dataframe, number,
list, and so on) that can be accessed by other functions. Let's have a look at an
example:

```
# prep data once and then pass around the program

passData <- reactive({
```

Some of the R code will be a little unfamiliar to you, but for now just concentrate
on what the program is actually doing. The first thing to note is that, unlike
previous examples, we are not making a call such as output$lineGraph
<- renderPlot({...}) or output$summaryText <- renderText({...}).
Instead, we are marking whatever is inside the call as *reactive* by enclosing it in
reactive({...}). This generates a reactive object called passData. This can
be accessed just like any other dataframe like this: passData() (for the whole
dataframe) or passData()$variableName (for a variable), or passData()[, 2:10]
(for the second to the tenth variable). Note the brackets after passData.

```
analytics <- analytics[analytics$Date %in%
              seq.Date(input$dateRange[1],
              input$dateRange[2], by = "days"),]
```

This command selects the dates that the user is interested in using the vector of two dates within `input$dateRange` as defined in `ui.R`. Note that the first of these dates is selected with `input$dateRange[1]` and the second with `input$dateRange[2]`. One of the nice things about this widget is it ensures users can only select logical values, that is, they can only select start dates that occur before end dates, and end dates that occur after start dates. Have a go and see. This keeps your code simpler because you know that only valid values will be returned (selection of the same date is possible, so your code will need to handle that case):

```
analytics <- analytics[analytics$Hour %in%
  as.numeric(input$minimumTime):
  as.numeric(input$maximumTime),]
```

This next instruction restricts the data to the requested time period. In this case, the user can select "wrong" values for the minimum and maximum time, with the maximum value being lower than the minimum value, because this part is made of two separate widgets. It doesn't affect the data extract in this case; the code will just match the sequence `10, 9, 8, 7, 6,` instead of the sequence `6, 7, 8, 9, 10,` so the data object is exactly the same. In a different application, you may need to check for the validity of the input or control the UI, so invalid selections are not possible. We will discuss the second possibility later on in the book:

```
if(class(input$domainShow)=="character") {
  analytics <- analytics[analytics$Domain %in%
    unlist(input$domainShow),]

}
```

And finally, the last statement restricts the data to either the NHS domain or the non-NHS domain according to user preference. The `if(){...}` statement checks to see if the user has made a selection before it subsets the data (an empty selection returns NULL, whereas any other selection will return an object of class character—a string, so that's what the code checks for). Quite often you will have to make sure that your code works with all the return types of the UI, or checks for valid input, whichever makes for the cleanest and simplest code:

```
analytics

})
```

We finish with the simple `analytics` instruction, which simply means "give `passData` the object **analytics**, which we've now defined as reactive based on the inputs in this instruction".

Outputs

Finally, the outputs are defined. Let's look first at the code that produces the first tab of output, monthly totals:

```
output$monthGraph <- renderPlot({

    graphData <- ddply(passData(), .(Domain, Date), numcolwise(sum))
```

The first instruction prepares the data using the user contributed package **plyr** (as with ggplot2, we have Hadley Wickham to thank for this package). This package is incredibly useful, but can be a little hard to understand at first. For now, just note that this instruction takes a dataframe as an input and then produces column sums based on unique combinations of domain and date. In this case, this means summing over the hours for each date or summing over the dates for each hour. This is the monthly graph, so we need to sum over the hours for each date. Instead of having 1 A.M. on the 21st, 2 A.M. on the 21st, 3 A.M. on the 21st, and so on, we just add them all up and have the totals for the 21st, the 22nd, and so on:

```
if(input$outputType == "visitors"){

    theGraph <- ggplot(graphData,
        aes(x = Date, y = visitors, group = Domain, colour = Domain))
        + geom_line() + ylab("Unique visitors")

}


if(input$outputType == "bounceRate"){

    theGraph <- ggplot(graphData,
        aes(x = Date, y = bounces / visits * 100, group = Domain,
        colour = Domain)) +
        geom_line() + ylab("Bounce rate %")

}


if(input$outputType == "timeOnSite"){

    theGraph <- ggplot(graphData,
        aes(x = Date, y = timeOnSite / visits, group = Domain,
        colour = Domain)) +
        geom_line() + ylab("Average time on site")

}
```

Following this we have three if({...}) statements that correspond to the three values of the radio button: total visitors, bounce rate, and time on site. Each of these instructions sets up a ggplot graph with the same parameters:

- Date on the x axis
- Grouping variable distinguished by color for the domain (this will draw a separate line for each domain and color them differently)
- A call to geom_line() to tell ggplot that we want a line graph

The only parameter that changes is y. This is the variable that will be shown on the graph, and is either equal simply to visitors (that is, number of visitors), bounces / visits * 100 (that is, the percentage of visitors who leave after the first page), or timeOnSite / visits (that is, the total time on site divided by the number of visits, to give the mean time on the site) and the ylab("...") argument that labels the y axis appropriately. Note that we have still not printed the graph anywhere, we are just setting it up.

```
if(input$smoother){

  theGraph <- theGraph + geom_smooth()

}
```

We can go on with the setup now with this instruction that checks to see if the user requested a smoothing line and, if they did, add one to the graph with geom_smooth().

```
print(theGraph)

})
```

Finally, we give the instruction to print() the graph. This is always necessary in ggplot-based graphics in Shiny, whether you have built up the graph in a separate variable or just given one instruction on one line. Don't forget this! It's a very common cause of problems, as you will no doubt notice if you spend any time on forums or mailing lists. Many newcomers make this mistake. The hourly graph is built up and outputted in exactly the same way, except using the hour variable in place of the date variable:

```
output$hourGraph <- renderPlot({

  graphData = ddply(passData(), .(Domain, Hour), numcolwise(sum))

  if(input$outputType == "visitors"){
```

```
    theGraph <- ggplot(graphData,
      aes(x = Hour, y = visitors, group = Domain,
      colour = Domain)) +
      geom_line() + ylab("Unique visitors")

  }

  if(input$outputType == "bounceRate"){

    theGraph <- ggplot(graphData,
      aes(x = Hour, y = bounces / visits * 100, group = Domain,
      colour = Domain)) +
      geom_line() + ylab("Bounce rate %")

  }

  if(input$outputType == "timeOnSite"){

    theGraph <- ggplot(graphData,
      aes(x = Hour, y = timeOnSite / visits, group = Domain,
      colour = Domain)) +
      geom_line() + ylab("Average time on site")

  }

  if(input$smoother){

    theGraph <- theGraph + geom_smooth()

  }

  print(theGraph)

})
```

Finally, the component that handles the text output runs as follows:

```
output$textDisplay <- renderText({
paste(
  length(seq.Date(input$dateRange[1], input$dateRange[2],
        by = "days")),
    " days are summarised. There were", sum(passData()$visitors),
    "visitors in this time period."
  )
})
```

You will be familiar with the `paste()` command by now; the first function within the `paste()` call produces a vector of dates between the two specified in the UI and then finds its length using, unsurprisingly, the `length()` command.

A note on the application code

Please note that, as at many points in this book, some of the decisions made around the `server.R` file were made to keep the code understandable and would not be used in a full application. The monthly and hourly graphics were drawn separately and each contained a data processing instruction at the beginning. A full application would do neither of these things. All data processing would be done in the first reactive call—producing either a list of two dataframes, one for each, or one larger frame that would feature values for both datasets. This makes the code easier to understand and maintain.

Further, although we have included two separate graph instructions and put them in different tabs, a full application would use one set of code that could handle both examples. Doing this requires a moderate level of proficiency with R. The code will be shorter, clearer, and easier to maintain, but more difficult to read and understand here if you are new to R.

Optional exercise

The Google Analytics application is reasonably intuitive and well featured (it doesn't, admittedly, compare all that favorably with Google's own offering!). However, as with the `server.R` code, some of the decisions around the UI setup were made for simplicity for the purposes of this book, to avoid flooding you with new widgets and ways of handling inputs in the second chapter. You may like to pause here and take a bit of time to update the code with some of the other UI elements Shiny offers to make the application function a bit more intuitive. Have a browse through the documentation yourself (`?shiny`) or make use of the following:

- `numericInput()`: This function gives both a textbox and a selection box to allow users to select a numeric value.
- `selectInput()`: This function allows a user to select one or multiple items from a list.
- `textInput()`: This function is not that useful in this case, but you can have some fun parsing its output with `as.numeric()` and using that as a numerical input

You will need to look at the return types for each of the widgets and make sure that the `server.R` code will accept them and, if not, change the code so that it will.

Those with some experience with R will no doubt be itching to fix the `server.R` file to clear up the issues outlined in the previous section. This will mainly sharpen your R skills and will also give you practice in some of the basics of scoping, classing, and passing data in a Shiny application. So if you feel up to it, have a go with this code too.

Summary

In this chapter we have covered a lot of ground. We've seen that Shiny applications are generally made up of two files: `server.R` and `ui.R`. We've learned what each part of the code does, including setting up `ui.R` with the position and type of inputs and outputs, and `server.R` with the data processing functions, outputs, and any reactive objects that are required.

The optional exercises have given you a chance to experiment with the code files in this chapter, varying the output types, using different widgets, and reviewing and adjusting their return values as appropriate. In addition, we've learned about the default layouts in Shiny, `pageWithSidebar()`, `mainPanel()`, and `tabsetPanel()`.

We've also learned about reactive objects and discussed when you might use reactive objects. There's more on finely controlling reactivity later in the book.

In the next chapter we're going to learn how to integrate Shiny with your own content, using HTML, CSS, and JavaScript.

3
Building Your Own Web Pages with Shiny

So, we've built our own application to query our site's data on Google Analytics. We've learned about the basic setup of a Shiny application and seen a lot of the widgets. It will be important to remember the majority of this basic structure because we are going to cover a lot of different territories in this chapter and, as a consequence, we won't have a single application at the end, like we did in the previous chapter. Instead, we will have lots of bits and pieces that you can use to start building your own content. Building one application with all of these different concepts would create several pages of code and it would be difficult to understand which part does what. As you go through the chapter, you might want to rebuild the Google Analytics application, or another of your own if you have one, using each of the concepts. If you do this, by the end you will have a beautifully styled and interactive application that you really understand. Or you might like to just browse through and pick out the things that you are particularly interested in; you should be able to understand each section on its own. Let's get started now. We are going to cover the following areas:

- Customizing Shiny applications, or whole web pages, using HTML
- Styling your Shiny application using CSS
- Turbo-charging your Shiny application with JavaScript and jQuery

Running the applications and code

For convenience, I have gathered together all the applications in this chapter. The link to the live versions as well as source code and data on my website can be found at http://chrisbeeley.net/website/shinybook.html. If you can, run the live version first, and then browse the code as you go through each example.

Shiny and HTML

It might seem quite intimidating to customize the HTML in a Shiny application, and you may feel that by going *under the hood*, it would be easy to break the application or ruin the styling. You may not want to bother rewriting every widget and output in HTML just to make one minor change to the interface.

In reality, Shiny is very accommodating, and you will find that it will quite happily accept a mix of Shiny and HTML code produced by you using Shiny helper functions, and the raw HTML written by you. So you can style just one button, or completely build the interface from scratch and integrate it with some other content. I'll show you all of these methods and provide some hints about the type of things you might like to do with them. Let's start simple by including some custom HTML in an otherwise vanilla Shiny application.

Custom HTML links in Shiny

This application makes use of data downloaded from a website I use a lot in my daily work, Patient Opinion (`www.patientopinion.org.uk/`). Patient Opinion lets users of health services tell their stories, and my organization makes extensive use of it to gather feedback about our services and improve them. This application uses data downloaded from the site and allows users to see the rate at which stories are posted that relate to different parts of the organization. On Patient Opinion, a custom HTML button will take the users straight from the application and onto the search page for that service area.

ui.R

Let's take a look at the `ui.R` first:

```
##################################
### custom HTML output - ui.R ###
##################################

library(shiny)

shinyUI(pageWithSidebar(

  headerPanel("Patient Opinion posts by area"),

  sidebarPanel(

    radioButtons("area", "Service area",
```

```
                  c("Armadillo", "Baboon",
                    "Camel", "Deer", "Elephant"),
                  selected = "Armadillo")
        ),

     mainPanel(
        h3("Total posts"),
        HTML("<p>Cumulative <em>totals</em> over time</p>"),
        plotOutput("plotDisplay"),
        htmlOutput("outputLink")
        )
  ))
```

Hopefully, you should remember the h3("...") function and all the other helper functions from the previous chapter. Just type ?p at the console for the full list. I have also included the HTML() function which marks text strings as HTML, avoiding the HTML escaping, which would otherwise render this on the screen verbatim.

The other new part of this file is the htmlOutput() function. This, like the HTML() function, prevents HTML escaping and allows you to use your own markup, but this time for text passed from server.R. Here's the final interface:

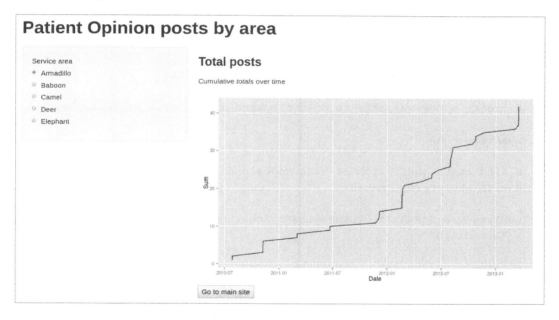

server.R

There are only a couple of new commands from Shiny in this example, so let's sharpen our R skills while we are here. The `server.R` file in this example, unlike many of the others in the book, deliberately does a lot of data management and clean-up at the top, before the reactive code. In this case, of course, I could have cleaned the data first and then loaded the clean data in the example. However, usually you will not have this luxury, either because results are loaded online from an API, or because your users will drop their own spreadsheets into the application folder, or some other reason such as this. So, let's look at a more realistic example and put aside Shiny commands for the moment.

server.R – data preparation

Let's look at the data preparation code first:

```
#########################################
##### custom HTML output - server.R ###
#########################################

library(shiny)
library(ggplot2)

# load the data- keeping strings as strings

PO <- read.csv("PO.csv", stringsAsFactors = FALSE)

# create a new variable to hold the area in and fill with blanks

PO$Area <- NA

# find posts that match service codes and label them
# with the correct names

PO$Area[grep("RHARY", PO$HealthServices, ignore.case=TRUE)] <-
  "Armadillo"

PO$Area[grep("RHAAR", PO$HealthServices, ignore.case=TRUE)] <-
  "Baboon"

PO$Area[grep("715", PO$HealthServices, ignore.case=TRUE)] <-
  "Camel"

PO$Area[grep("710i", PO$HealthServices, ignore.case=TRUE)] <-
```

```
    "Deer"

PO$Area[grep("700", PO$HealthServices, ignore.case=TRUE)] <-
    "Elephant"

# create a postings variable to add together for a
# cumulative sum- give it 1

PO$ToAdd <- 1

# remove all missing values for Area
# (since they will never be shown)

PO <- PO[!is.na(PO$Area),]

# API returns data in reverse chronological order- reverse it

PO <- PO[nrow(PO):1,]

# produce cumulative sum column

PO$Sum <- ave(PO$ToAdd, PO$Area, FUN = cumsum)

# produce a date column from the data column in the spreadsheet

PO$Date <- as.Date(substr(PO$dtSubmitted, 1, 10),
            format = "%Y-%m-%d")
```

After loading the Shiny package and any other packages that are necessary, a comma delimited spreadsheet (`.csv`) is loaded with the `read.csv()` command. You may often want to use `stringsAsFactors` = `FALSE`. Factor is a special class in R which is useful for statistical applications. A full discussion on the properties of the factor class is rather outside the scope of this book. For now, it is sufficient to say that if you have any strings in your spreadsheet that you want to treat as strings (for example, extracting characters, coercing other variable types such as date, and so on), do ensure that you import them as strings and not as factors as done in the previous example. If you want to use factors for certain particular variables (particularly for ggplot2 which can require factors for some arguments), you can always coerce them later on. Data preparation proceeds as follows:

- A new variable is created and filled with R's missing data value, NA. The missing data value is of great use in a lot of R code; here we are using it so that we can easily discard all the datapoints that fail to match to areas.

- The subset operator `[]` is then used with the `grep()` command (familiar to Unix-like OS users and which returns the positions of a character vector matching a search string). This marks all the rows of the newly created empty variable that matches each service code with a name that is meaningful to the end users.

- A helper variable `ToAdd` is then given a value of `1` for all the rows. This will be used to calculate the cumulative total of posts for each area.

- `PO[!is.na(PO$Area),]` is used to return all the rows of the dataset that do not have missing values for the area variable (that is, failed to match). `!is.na(x)` is a useful function that returns the positions of all the non-missing values of x.

- The API for the website returns the data in reverse chronological order, so it is flipped over using the row indices `nrow(PO):1`, that is, a sequence of integers starting at the number of rows of the data and going down to 1.

- The `ave()` function is used to return the cumulative sum (`cumsum`) for each grouping (`PO$Area`).

- The date string (which has the time appended) is shrunk to the correct size using `substr()` and coerced to R's date class using `as.Date()`. The date class can often trip up newcomers, so it is worth having a good read of `?as.Date()`. Coercing a character string and not a factor, and ensuring that you specify the format of the string properly, should get you over the common pitfalls.

Again, don't worry too much if you don't follow all of the R code. Learning R is really a book in itself. I've included it here to help you get used to the kind of things that you might want to do, and to show you the commonly used shortcuts and pitfalls for beginners. Let's have a look at the `server.R` file.

server.R – server definition

This file produces a plot of the cumulative totals of postings and produces a nicely formatted HTML button ready to post straight into the UI:

```
shinyServer(function(input, output) {

  output$plotDisplay <- renderPlot({

    # select only the area as selected in the UI

    toPlot = PO[PO$Area == input$area,]

    print(
      ggplot(toPlot, aes(x = Date, y = Sum)) + geom_line()
```

```
    )

})

output$outputLink <- renderText({

   # switch command in R as in many other programming languages

   link <- switch(input$area,
                  "Armadillo" =
     "http://www.patientopinion.org.uk/services/rhary",
                  "Baboon" =
     "http://www.patientopinion.org.uk/services/rhaar",
                  "Camel" =
     "http://www.patientopinion.org.uk/services/rha_715",
                  "Deer" =
     "http://www.patientopinion.org.uk/services/rha_710i",
                  "Elephant" =
     "http://www.patientopinion.org.uk/services/rha_700"
   )

   # paste the HTML together

   paste0('<form action="', link, '"target="_blank">
          <input type="submit" value="Go to main site">
          </form>')
 })
})
```

You can see the subsetting again carried out with our old friend [] and a ggplot() call in the plot function. Just remember to wrap it in print() (as done in the previous chapter).

The HTML button is created very easily using the switch() command, and paste0() which concatenates strings with no spaces. With that, our newly created object output$ouputLink is ready to be sent straight to the UI and included as raw HTML.

Minimal HTML interface

Now that we have dipped our toes into HTML, let's build a (nearly) minimal example of an interface entirely in HTML. To use your own HTML in a Shiny application, create the server.R file as you normally would. Then, instead of a ui.R file, create a folder called www and place a file called index.html inside this folder. This is where you will define your interface.

index.html

Let's look at each chunk of `index.html` in turn:

```
<!---------------------------->
<!--Minimal example- HTML UI -->
<!---------------------------->

<html>

<head>
  <title>HTML minimal example</title>
  <script src="shared/jquery.js" type="text/javascript"></script>
  <script src="shared/shiny.js" type="text/javascript"></script>
  <link rel="stylesheet" type="text/css" href="shared/shiny.css"/>
  <style type = "text/css">
    body {
      background-color: #ecf1ef;
    }

    #navigation {
      position: absolute;
      width: 300px;
    }

    #centerdoc {
      max-width: 600px;
      margin-left: 350px;
      border-left: 1px solid #c6ec8c;
      padding-left: 20px;
    }
  </style>

</head>
```

The `<head>` section contains some important setup for Shiny, loading the JavaScript and jQuery scripts which make it work, as well as a stylesheet for Shiny. You will need to add some CSS of your own unless you want every element of the interface and output to be displayed as a big list down the screen, and the whole thing to look very ugly. For simplicity, I've added some very basic CSS in the `<head>` section; you could, of course, use a separate CSS file and add a link to it just as `shiny.css` is referenced.

The body of the HTML contains all the input and output elements that you want to use, and any other content that you want on the page. In this case, I've mixed up a Shiny interface with a picture of my cats, because no web page is complete without a picture of a cat! Have a look at the following code:

```html
<body>

  <h1>Minimal HTML UI</h1>

  <div id = "navigation">

    <p>
      <label>Title for graph:</label><br />
      <textarea name="comment" rows = "4"
      cols = "30">My first graph</textarea>
    </p>

    <p>
      <label>What sort of graph would you like?</label><br />
      <input type="radio" name="graph"
      value="1" title="Straight line" checked>Linear<br>
      <input type="radio" name="graph" value="2"
      title="Curve" >Quadratic<br>
    </p>

      <label>Here's a picture of my cats</label><br />
      <img src="cat.jpg" alt="My cats"
      width="300" height = "300">

  </div>

  <div id = "centerdoc">

    <div id="textDisplay" class="shiny-text-output"></div>
    <br/ >

    <div id="plotDisplay" class="shiny-plot-output"
    style="width: 80%; height: 400px"></div>

  </div>

</body>

</html>
```

There are three main elements: a title and two `<div>` sections, one for the UI and one for the output. The UI is defined within the navigation `<div>`, which is left aligned. Recreating Shiny widgets in HTML is pretty simple and you can also use HTML elements that are not given in Shiny. Instead of replacing the `textInput()` widget with `<input type="text">` (which is equivalent), I have instead used `<textarea>`, which allows more control over the size and shape of the input area.

The `radioButtons()` widget can be recreated with `<input type = "radio">`. You can see that both get a name attribute, which is referenced in the `server.R` file as `input$name` (in this case, `input$comment` and `input$graph`). Another advantage of using your own HTML is you can add tooltips; I have added these to the radio buttons using the `title` attribute.

The output region is set up with two `<div>` tags: one which is named `textDisplay` and picks up `output$textDisplay` as defined in `server.R`; and the other which is named `plotDisplay` and picks up `output$plotDisplay` from the `server.R` file. In your own code, you will need to specify the class as shown in the previous example, as either `shiny-text-output` (for text), `shiny-plot-output` (for plots), or `shiny-html-output` (for tables or anything else that R will output as HTML). You will need to specify the height of plots (in px, cm, and so on) and can optionally specify width either in absolute or relative (%) terms.

Just to demonstrate that you can throw anything in there that you like, there's a picture of my cats underneath the UI. You will, of course, have something a bit more sophisticated in mind. Add more `<div>` sections, links, pictures and just whatever you like.

server.R

Let us have a quick look at the `server.R` file:

```
################################################
##### minimal example for HTML- server.R #####
################################################

library(shiny)

shinyServer(function(input, output) {

  output$textDisplay <- renderText({

    paste0("Title:'", input$comment,
```

```
            "'. There are ", nchar(input$comment),
            " characters in this."
      )
  })


  output$plotDisplay <- renderPlot({

    par(bg = "#ecf1ef") # set the background color

    plot(poly(1:100, as.numeric(input$graph)), type = "l",
      ylab="y", xlab="x")

  })


})
```

Text handling is done as before. You'll notice that the renderPlot() function begins by setting the background color to the same as the page itself (par(bg = "#ecf1ef") and for more graphical options in R, see ?par). You don't have to do this, but the graph's background will be visible as a big white square if you don't. The next chapter will tell you how to draw your graph as a **png** and handle the transparency yourself.

The actual plot itself uses the poly() command to produce a set of numbers from a linear or quadratic function according to the user input (that is, input$graph). Note the use of as.numeric() to coerce the value we get from the radio button definition in index.html from a string to a number. This is a common source of error in Shiny code and you must remember to keep track of how variables are stored, whether as lists, strings, or other variable types; and either coerce them into place (as done here), or coerce them all in one go using a reactive function. The latter option can be a good idea to make your code less fiddly and buggy, since it removes the need to keep track of variable types in every single function you write. There is more about defining your own reactive functions and passing data around a Shiny instance in the next chapter. The type ="l" argument returns a line graph, and the xlab and ylab arguments give labels to the x and y axes.

The following screenshot shows the finished article:

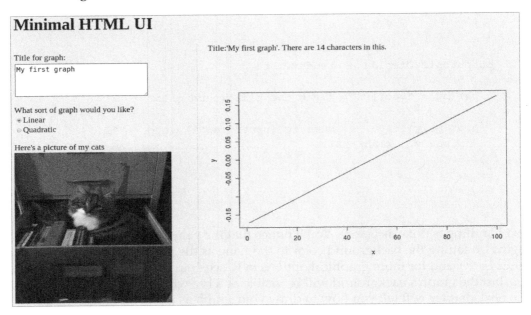

JavaScript and Shiny

With Shiny, JavaScript, and jQuery, you can build pretty much anything you can think of; moreover, Shiny and jQuery will do a lot of the heavy lifting which means fairly minimal amounts of code will be required. We are going to have a look at another couple of *toy* examples. Firstly, we will look at using JavaScript to manipulate the inputs of a Shiny application, and then at using jQuery to manipulate the outputs. Please note that these examples do not represent the best practice in coding as they do not make the best use of CSS, HTML, or jQuery. They are just there to demonstrate the principles and show you how easy it is. In your own applications, you will need to make use of HTML, JavaScript (and/or jQuery), and CSS in the most appropriate and efficient way.

ui.R

This example also includes more examples related to including custom HTML without writing the whole thing out in HTML yourself. Let's have a look at the ui.R file:

```
################################################
#### Animating text with JavaScript- ui.R #####
################################################
```

```
library(shiny)

shinyUI(pageWithSidebar(
  headerPanel("Text based animations"),

  sidebarPanel(
    h3("Let's animate something!"),          # heading helper
    p("Please enjoy the
      animation responsibly"),               # paragraph helper
    tags$textarea(id="textArea",             # tags$XX for
                  "Please enter text here"), # generating HTML
    tags$input(type = "button",
               id = "animate",
               value = "Animate!",
               onClick = "buttonClick()")    # reference to JS
  ),

  mainPanel(
    tags$canvas(id="myCanvas", # graphical output area
                width="500",
                height="250"),
    includeHTML("textSend.js"), # include JS file
    textOutput("textDisplay")
  )
))
```

There are two things in this file that you haven't seen before. The first
is the `tags$xxx()` function which will generate HTML for you. The
`tags$textarea(id="textArea", "Please enter text here")` call generates the
following:

```
<textarea id="textArea" class="shiny-bound-input">Please enter text
here</textarea>.
```

Similarly, the whole `tags$input(...)` call generates the following:

```
<input type="button" id="animate" value="Animate!"
onclick="buttonClick()">.
```

The second thing that you haven't seen before is the `includeHTML()` function. This
allows you to link to a file that contains a lot of HTML (in this case, a JavaScript
definition), rather than cluttering up your `ui.R` with it. You could very well include
plain HTML using this function.

server.R

The `server.R` file is unchanged from our original minimal example:

```
####################################################
##### Animating text with JavaScript - server.R ####
####################################################

library(shiny)

shinyServer(function(input, output) {

  output$textDisplay <- renderText({ # handle Shiny
                                     # text function
    paste0("You said '", input$textArea,
           "'. There are ", nchar(input$textArea),
           " characters in this."
    )
  })
})
```

Of course, you can do much more processing than this if you wish. The JavaScript file contains no surprises, and functions just as it does in any other web application:

```
<script type="text/javascript">

function buttonClick(){

  // get and set up the drawing canvas

  var c=document.getElementById("myCanvas");
  var ctx=c.getContext("2d");
  ctx.font="30px Arial";

  // get the text from the UI

  var text = document.getElementById("textArea").value;

  // set up positional variables

  var textX = 150;
  var textY = 1;

  // define move function
```

```
function move(){

    ctx.clearRect(0, 0, c.width, c.height);
    ctx.fillText(text, textX, textY * 5);

    if(textY++ < 40){

        setTimeout(move, 25); // delay between frames
    }
}

move(); // call function
}

</script>
```

We won't look in detail at the JavaScript because that is rather out of the scope of this discussion. The important things to note are the first code chunk, which picks up the drawing canvas we drew in the ui.R file and sets it up; and the second code chunk, which picks up the input from the textarea that we defined in ui.R. The rest of the code just draws the text on the screen and then animates it so that it falls down the frame. Here is the screenshot that displays it:

You will, I am sure, wish to produce something a little more sophisticated than this!

jQuery

For the ultimate quick and clean code, let's add some jQuery. We are going to add mouseover row highlighting (that is, coloring in the rows of a table when the mouse pointer is on them) for a table from Shiny (this can be done in CSS, of course, but this is just an example) and allow the user to bold individual cells by clicking on them, as well as producing a pop-up information box about the dataset.

index.html – body

We'll skip the head for now and look at the body of the index.html file:

```html
<body>
    <h1>jQuery example</h1>

    <div id = "navigation">

      <label for="dataSet">Select dataset</label>
      <select id="dataSet">
        <option value="iris" selected="selected">
          Iris data</option>
        <option value="USPersonalExpenditure">
          Personal expenditure data</option>
        <option value="CO2">CO2 data</option>
      </select>

    </div>

    <div id = "centerdoc">

      <div id="datatext" class="shiny-text-output"></div>

      <div id="hiddentext" style = "text-indent: 100%;
        white-space: nowrap; overflow: hidden"
        class="shiny-text-output">
      </div>

      <div id="dataset" class="shiny-html-output"></div>

    </div>

</body>
```

The interface, as you can see, allows users to select one of three datasets which are included in R. There are two outputs that are visible, which are some text followed by a table that will be specified within the server.R file (you can see them in the previous code snippet, the <div> sections with id = "datatext" and id = "dataset"). A further <div> section (with id = "hiddentext") allows R to generate some text, so make it available to jQuery but without displaying it on the screen until the user requests it. Let's now look at the server.R file.

server.R

Following is the server.R file:

```
library(shiny)

shinyServer(function(input, output) {

  output$dataset <- renderTable({

    theData = switch(input$dataSet,
                     "iris" = iris,
                     "USPersonalExpenditure" =
                         USPersonalExpenditure,
                     "CO2" = CO2)

  head(theData)

  })

  output$datatext <- renderText({

    paste0("This is the ", input$dataSet, " dataset")

  })

  output$hiddentext <- renderText({

    paste0("Dataset has ", nrow(switch(input$dataSet,
                          "iris" = iris,
                          "USPersonalExpenditure" =
                          USPersonalExpenditure,
                          "CO2" = CO2)), " rows")

  })
})
```

The function within `renderTable()` quite simply takes the string sent from the interface and returns the dataset within R with the same name. It then displays the first few rows of the dataset using `head()`, which is returned as an HTML table. There are two calls made to `renderText()`, as can be seen. The first returns a text string describing which dataset has been selected. The second returns a description of the number of rows in the dataset. This will be hidden from the user and is only accessible via jQuery. Before we go into detail, here is the finished interface:

jQuery example

Select dataset	Iris data	▾	This is the iris dataset				
				Sepal.Length	Sepal.Width	Petal.Length	Petal.Width	Species
			1	5.10	3.50	1.40	0.20 setosa
			2	4.90	3.00	1.40	0.20 setosa
			3	**4.70**	3.20	1.30	0.20 setosa
			4	4.60	3.10	1.50	0.20 setosa
			5	5.00	3.60	1.40	0.20 setosa
			6	5.40	3.90	1.70	0.40 setosa

As you can see in the previous screenshot, the first row is highlighted. This is achieved through a mouseover (which works on any row). The third value of `Sepal.Length` is in bold and this is achieved through a mouse click. Double clicking on the text above the table brings up a message about the dataset, as shown in the following screenshot:

This, of course, is the text that we generated and hid, as we saw in the `server.R` and `index.html` files. Let's look at the jQuery to do this.

jQuery

Like before, you can keep the jQuery code wherever you like: in a text file, verbatim in the `<head>` of your html, or using a call to `includeHTML()` from a `ui.R` file. As usual, wrap your code in the following manner:

```
$(document).ready(function(){
  ...
})
```

Please have a look at the piece of code in standard jQuery:

```
$('tr').mouseover(function(){
    $(this).css('background-color', 'yellow');
});
```

This will not work because your output will be redrawn, and so you will need to access all the elements that will be drawn as well as those that already are. Rewrite the previous code in the following manner (it is a piece of code from Joe Cheng of RStudio):

```
$(document).on("mouseover", "tr", function(evt) {
  $(this).css('background-color', 'yellow');
})
```

The previous is the `mouseover` code that handles row highlighting, and following is the `mouseout` code to put it back to normal once the pointer leaves:

```
$(document).on("mouseout", "tr", function(evt) {
  $(this).css('background-color', 'transparent');
});
```

Applying bold effects to individual cells is achieved through the following code snippet. As you can see, the function starts by clearing bold formatting from all the cells (in case a different cell has already been highlighted by the user) and then bolds the cell that has been clicked:

```
$(document).on("click", "td", function(evt) {
  $('td').css('font-weight', 'normal');
  $(this).css('font-weight', 'bold');
})
```

Lastly, the following code snippet describes a function that listens for a double-click on the text that describes the dataset, and then gives more information about the data, which we have placed on the screen and hidden:

```
$(document).on("dblclick", "#datatext", function(evt) {
  alert($('#hiddentext').text());
})
```

As with the JavaScript example, none of these functions are going to win any prizes for UI design, but they do hopefully illustrate some general things that are very easy to accomplish. Following are some examples of things you might like to try in your own applications:

- Click to expand sets of rows in large tables

- Custom highlighting of table cells within a user-set range (note that this can be done without jQuery, using pure Shiny code, but it is more difficult this way)

- Mouseover help text to provide additional documentation for a Shiny application

Exercise

If you haven't already been tempted, now is definitely a good time to have a go at building your own application with your own data. The next chapter covers advanced topics in Shiny and, though you are welcome to plough on, a little practical experience with the functions will stand you in good stead for the next chapter. If you're interested in sharing your creations right away, feel free to jump to *Chapter 5, Running and Sharing Your Creations*.

How you go about building your first application will very much depend on your previous experience and what you want to achieve with Shiny, but as with everything in life, it is better to start simple. Start with the minimal example given in the previous chapter and put in some data that's relevant to you. Shiny applications can be hard to debug (compared to interactive R sessions, at least), so in your early forays, keep things very simple. For example, instead of drawing a graph, start with a simple `renderText()` call and just print the first few values of a variable. This will, at least, let you know that your data is loading okay and the server and UI are communicating properly. Always make sure that any code you write in R (graphs, tables, data management, and so on) works in a plain interactive session, before you put it into a Shiny application!

Probably the most helpful and simple debugging technique is to use `cat()` to print to the R console. There are two main reasons why you should do this. The first is to put in little messages to yourself, for example, `cat("This branch of code executed")`. The second is to print the properties of R objects if you are having problems relating to data structure, size, or type. `cat(str(x))` is particularly useful and will print a summary of any kind of R object, whether it is a list, a dataframe, a numeric vector, or anything else.

The other useful method is a standard method of debugging in R, `browser()`, which can be put anywhere in your code. As soon as it is executed, it halts the application and enters the debug mode (see `?browser`).

Once you have the application working, you can start to add custom HTML using Shiny's built-in functions or rewrite ui.R into index.html. The choice here really depends on how much HTML you want to include. Although, in theory, you can create very large HTML interfaces in Shiny using .html files referenced by the includeHTML() command, you will end up with a rather confusing list of markups scattered across different files. Rewriting to raw HTML is likely to be the easier option in most cases. If you are already proficient in JavaScript and/or jQuery, then you may like to have a go at using them with a Shiny application. If not, you can leave this for now or perhaps just modify the code included in this chapter to see whether you can get different and interesting effects.

Summary

This chapter has put quite a heap of tools in your Shiny toolbox. You have learned how to use custom HTML straight from a minimal ui.R UI setup, and how to build the whole thing from scratch using HTML and CSS. You have also looked at some data management and cleaning in R, and at some examples of Shiny applications using JavaScript and jQuery. Hopefully, by now, you should have made your own application, whether in pure Shiny or with your own HTML markup, and perhaps experimented with JavaScript/jQuery. In the next chapter, we are going to learn more about higher control over Shiny applications, including controlling reactivity, scoping and passing variables, and a variety of input/output functions.

4
Taking Control of Reactivity, Inputs, and Outputs

So far in this book we've mastered the basics of Shiny by building our own Google Analytics (GA) application, as well as looked at how to style and extend Shiny applications using HTML, CSS, and JavaScript. In this chapter we are going to extend our toolkit by learning about advanced Shiny functions. These allow you to take control of the fine details of your application, including the interface, reactivity, data, and graphics.

In order to do this, we're going to go back to the Google Analytics application and totally upgrade it, making it much smoother, more intuitive, and well-featured. The finished code and data for this advanced GA application can be found at `https://github.com/ChrisBeeley/GoogleAnalyticsAdvanced`.

In this chapter we will do the following:

- Learn how to show and hide parts of the interface
- Change the interface reactively
- Finely control reactivity so functions and outputs run at the appropriate time
- Use URLs and reactive Shiny functions to populate and alter the selections within an interface
- Upload and download data to and from a Shiny application
- Use custom graphics and animations in Shiny

Showing and hiding elements of the UI

We'll start easy with a simple function that you are certainly going to need if you build even a moderately complex application. Those of you who have been doing extra credit exercises and/or experimenting with your own applications will probably have already wished for this or, indeed, have already found it. `conditionalPanel()` allows you to show/hide UI elements based on other selections within the UI. The function takes a condition (in JavaScript, but the form and syntax will be familiar from many languages) and a UI element, and displays the UI only when the condition is true. This is actually used a couple of times in the advanced GA application and indeed in all the applications I've ever written of even moderate complexity. The following is a simpler example (from ui.R, of course, in the first section, within `sidebarPanel()`), which allows users who request a smoothing line to decide what type they want:

```
conditionalPanel(
  condition = "input.smoother == true",
  selectInput("linearModel", "Linear or smoothed",
              list("lm", "loess"))
)
```

As you can see, the condition appears very R/Shiny-like, except with the "." operator familiar to JavaScript users in place of "$", and with "true" in lower case. This is a very simple but powerful way of making sure that your UI is not cluttered with irrelevant material.

Giving names to tabPanel elements

In order to further streamline the UI, we're going to hide the hour selector when the monthly graph is displayed and the date selector when the hourly graph is displayed. The difference is illustrated in the following screenshot with side-by-side pictures, hourly figures UI on the left-hand side and monthly figures on the right-hand side:

In order to do this, we're going to have to first give the tabs of the tabbed output names. This is done as follows (with the new code in bold):

```
tabsetPanel(id ="theTabs",
            tabPanel("Summary", textOutput("textDisplay"),
              value = "summary"),
            tabPanel("Monthly figures",
              plotOutput("monthGraph"), value = "monthly"),
            tabPanel("Hourly figures",
              plotOutput("hourGraph"), value = "hourly")
    )
```

As you can see, the whole panel is given an ID (theTabs), and then each tabPanel is also given a name (summary, monthly, and hourly). They are referred to in the server.R file very simply as input$theTabs. Let's have a quick look at a chunk of code in server.R that references the tab names; this code makes sure that we subset based on date only when the date selector is actually visible, and by hour only when the hour selector is actually visible. Our function to calculate and pass data now looks like the following (new code again bolded):

```
passData <- reactive({

if(input$theTabs != "hourly"){

    analytics <- analytics[analytics$Date %in%
```

```
        seq.Date(input$dateRange[1], input$dateRange[2],
          by = "days"),]

}

if(input$theTabs != "monthly"){

  analytics <- analytics[analytics$Hour %in%
                as.numeric(input$minimumTime) :
                as.numeric(input$maximumTime),]

}

analytics <- analytics[analytics$Domain %in%
              unlist(input$domainShow),]

analytics

})
```

As you can see, subsetting by month is carried out only when the date display is visible (that is, when the hourly tab is not shown), and vice versa.

Finally, we can make our changes to ui.R to remove parts of the UI based on tab selection:

```
conditionalPanel(
  condition = "input.theTabs != 'hourly'",
  dateRangeInput(inputId = "dateRange",
                label = "Date range",
                start = "2013-04-01",
                max = Sys.Date()
  )
),

conditionalPanel(
  condition = "input.theTabs != 'monthly'",
  sliderInput(inputId = "minimumTime",
              label = "Hours of interest- minimum",
              min = 0,
              max = 23,
              value = 0,
```

```
                    step = 1
    ),

    sliderInput(inputId = "maximumTime",
                label = "Hours of interest- maximum",
                min = 0,
                max = 23,
                value = 23,
                step = 1)
    )
```

Note the use in the latter example of two UI elements within the same `conditionalPanel()` call; it is worth noting that it helps you keep your code clean and easy to debug.

Reactive user interfaces

Another trick you will definitely want up your sleeve at some point is a reactive user interface. This enables you to change your UI (for example, the number or content of radio buttons) based on reactive functions. For example, consider an application that I wrote related to survey responses across a broad range of health services in different areas. The services are related to each other in quite a complex hierarchy, and over time, different areas and services respond (or cease to exist, or merge, or change their name...), which means that for each time period the user might be interested in, there would be a totally different set of areas and services. The only sensible solution to this problem is to have the user tell you which area and date range they are interested in and then give them back the correct list of services that have survey responses within that area and date range.

The example we're going to look at is a little simpler than this, just to keep from getting bogged down in too much detail, but the principle is exactly the same and you should not find this idea too difficult to adapt to your own UI. We are going to imagine that your users are interested in the individual domains from which people are accessing the site, rather than just have them lumped together as the NHS domain and all others. To this end, we will have a combo box with each individual domain listed. This combo box is likely to contain a very high number of domains across the whole time range, so we will let users constrain the data by date and only have the domains that feature in that range return. Not the most realistic example, but it will illustrate the principle for our purposes.

Reactive user interface example – server.R

The big difference is that instead of writing your UI definition in your ui.R file, you place it in server.R, and wrap it in renderUI(). Then all you do is point to it from your ui.R file. Let's have a look at the relevant bit of the server.R file:

```
output$reacDomains <- renderUI({

    domainList = unique(as.character(passData()$networkDomain))

    selectInput("subDomains", "Choose subdomain", domainList)

})
```

The first line takes the reactive dataset that contains only the data between the dates selected by the user and gives all the unique values of domains within it. The second line is a widget type we have not used yet which generates a combo box. The usual id and label arguments are given, followed by the values that the combo box can take. This is taken from the variable defined in the first line.

Reactive user interface example – ui.R

The ui.R file merely needs to point to the reactive definition as shown in the following line of code (just add it in to the list of widgets within sidebarPanel()):

```
uiOutput("reacDomains")
```

You can now point to the value of the widget in the usual way, as input$subDomains. Note that you do *not* use the name as defined in the call to renderUI(), that is, reacDomains, but rather the name as defined within it, that is, subDomains.

Advanced reactivity

Now that we've warmed up a bit, let's discuss reactivity in a bit more detail. As we've already learned, reactive functions and objects automatically take dependencies on their inputs. We've also seen that it's often a good idea to use reactive objects rather than just output functions because data objects can be created once and then passed around to different output functions. We're now going to discuss, in a bit more detail, the use of reactive objects in Shiny as well as special functions within it to control reactivity. There is more about reactivity and some very helpful diagrams on the Shiny tutorial pages at http://rstudio.github.io/shiny/tutorial/#reactivity-overview.

The default behavior, as we have seen throughout the book, handles quite a lot of different applications. However, sometimes the default behavior will be slow or confusing for users of your application, or will result in code that is hard to write or maintain or even just not useful. Along with using reactive objects within Shiny, there are special functions that you can use to take control of inputs and outputs to Shiny applications. I'll summarize them briefly and then show a use case for each one within the Google Analytics application.

The `submitButton()` and `isolate()` functions are both used in cases where data is slow to get or process. In essence, they allow you to control when Shiny processes information from a dependency. So, for example, if your data processing instruction takes 10 seconds to run, users won't mind waiting a few times, but they don't want to wait every time they click on a button. The `submitButton()` controls the whole interface, and no reactive processing is carried out until it has been pushed by the user. The `isolate()` function is a little more subtle than this and allows you to prevent reactive objects and functions from forming dependencies on individual inputs. Essentially, it prevents a costly rerun of data processing or output every time irrelevant changes are made on the UI and gives a smoother experience for your user.

Another weapon in your reactivity arsenal is `invalidateLater()`, which allows you to make an object reactive, not on the basis of user inputs but rather on the passing of time. An obvious example would be a financial information application, which is refreshed every minute on a server to which the application has access. The outputs can be kept up-to-date even when the user is not interacting with the application using the `invalidateLater()` function.

Let's have a closer look at each of these methods in turn.

Using reactive objects and functions efficiently

As we've already seen, using a reactive object is a good idea to save from having to maintain several chunks of code that all do the same thing (typically, prepare your data based on user inputs). Another time you might want to use reactive objects is if your reactive function is inefficient or slow. Sometimes a reactive object is a good idea if you have a lot of complicated inputs that need coercing to different variable types; it's easier to produce a nice, clean, simple R object with all the correct variable types in it than to write lots of horrible `as.character(input$variable)` calls all over the place and remember in what variable type everything is.

So, for example, I did some fiddling with the output of the widgets to build the widget browser presented in *Chapter 2, Building Your First Application*, in order to fit all the different output types in one column (browse back to *Chapter 2* to have a look, use `runGist(6571951)` to run the application, or refer to `https://gist.github.com/ChrisBeeley/6571951` for the code). This was fine for this one example, but if I had needed the output elsewhere in the application again, I certainly would not like to write and maintain code to remake it from the inputs every time. It is much easier to just build the object once, place it in a reactive object, and then call on it wherever you need it.

Controlling the whole interface with the submitButton() function

This is easily the simplest approach to dealing with a lot of the problems that you might encounter with slow reactive functions. The `submitButton()` function allows you to include a button on your UI which ensures that no functions run at all until the button is clicked. The same reactive dependencies are taken by output functions, so the programming is just as simple, but the users can take their time selecting the right inputs before the long computation for the outputs begins. Place the following into a UI definition:

```
submitButton(text = "Produce output")
```

That's it! Although a wonderfully simple method, in some circumstances it would be overkill, and takes away the feeling of interactivity even when the user is making minor changes to the output (the title of a graph, for example). Shiny does give you finer control than this, should you need it. This is achieved with the `isolate()` function.

Controlling specific inputs with the isolate() function

The `isolate()` function allows you to take particular parts of the input and break the dependency that they would otherwise form with reactive functions. For example, you might wish your call to the Google Analytics API to be reactive so that it is kept constantly up-to-date. However, you do not want to make a request to the API every time something tiny changes because it will slow down the whole application waiting for the results to download and putting them into the right format to be analyzed. In this case, you might wish to have the data re-download every time the user changes the hours that they are interested in (which suggests an interest in real-time data), but not every time they do anything else, such as change the date range or whether they want the "NHS" or "Other" domain.

In order to do this we will set up another data function that downloads data from the API every time.

We did not cover using the Google Analytics API in detail in *Chapter 2, Building Your First Application,* and won't here either because it can be a bit fiddly to use and will distract from what we are doing. This code makes use of the rga package mentioned in *Chapter 2, Building Your First Application* and will re-download the data every time the user changes their hourly range. Note that my username and password have been replaced with xxxx, you can get your own user details from the Google Analytics website. Note also that this code is not included on the GitHub because it requires the username and password to be present in order for it to work:

```
# open a connection in the preamble to the application
rga.open(instance = "ga", where="ga.rga",
         client.id = "XXXX.apps.googleusercontent.com",
         client.secret = "XXXX")
# download a copy at application startup

analytics <- ga$getData(XXXX, batch = TRUE,
           start.date = "2013-05-01",
           metrics = "ga:visitors, ga:visits,
           ga:bounces, ga:timeOnSite",
           dimensions = "ga:dateHour, ga:networkDomain",
           sort = "", filters = "", segment = "")


# define the shinyServer()
shinyServer(function(input, output){
...

  hourlyData <- reactive({

  # download fresh data from server
  analytics <- ga$getData(XXXX, batch = TRUE,
             start.date = "2013-05-01",
             metrics = "ga:visitors, ga:visits,
             ga:bounces, ga:timeOnSite",
             dimensions = "ga:dateHour, ga:networkDomain",
             sort = "", filters = "", segment = "")

  # form a dependency on input$minimumTime and input$maximumTime
    analytics <- analytics[analytics$Hour %in%
                 as.numeric(input$minimumTime) :
                 as.numeric(input$maximumTime),]
```

```
    # avoid dependency on data and domain
    analytics <- isolate({
      analytics[analytics$Date %in% seq.Date(input$dateRange[1],
        input$dateRange[2], by = "days"),]

      analytics <- analytics[analytics$Domain %in%
        unlist(input$domainShow),]

    })

    analytics

  })
… # rest of shinyServer({}) call
```

This is a somewhat contrived example, of course, because you now have two copies of the data in the application, one right up to the minute and one downloaded when the application started up. It does illustrate the basic point of isolating slow or otherwise expensive code in order to keep your application responsive where it needs to be.

Running reactive functions over time

If your users want to be kept really up-to-the-minute with the Google Analytics data, data can be downloaded pretty much in real-time with the invalidateLater() command. The invalidateLater() command causes reactive functions to re-execute after a certain period of time has elapsed. Note that the invalidateLater() function takes a session argument. This is used in some of Shiny's advanced functions. Simply give the shinyServer() call a session argument (shinyServer(function(input, output, session) {}) and then add in the argument wherever necessary in the rest of your code. The documentation (which can be found by entering ?shiny at the console—as a reminder, accessing help files this way is represented in this book simply as ?shiny, ?ggplot, and so on) will make clear which functions require a session argument. It seems likely that more will be added beyond the current version of Shiny, which is 0.60 at the time of writing.

The other argument that invalidateLater() takes is the number of milliseconds you wish to elapse before the function is called again. We can rewrite the data function using invalidateLater() in the following manner:

```
hourlyData <- reactive({

  # schedule the reactive context to re-execute in 10 seconds

  invalidateLater(10000, session)
```

```
# download fresh data from server
analytics <- ga$getData(XXXX, batch = TRUE,
                  start.date = "2013-05-01",
                  metrics = "ga:visitors, ga:visits,
                  ga:bounces, ga:timeOnSite",
                  dimensions = "ga:dateHour,
                  ga:networkDomain",
                  sort = "", filters = "", segment = "")

# use isolate to avoid other dependencies

analytics <- isolate({

  analytics <- analytics[analytics$Hour %in%
              as.numeric(input$minimumTime) :
              as.numeric(input$maximumTime),]

  analytics <- analytics[analytics$Date %in%
              seq.Date(input$dateRange[1],
              input$dateRange[2], by = "days"),]

  analytics <- analytics[analytics$Domain %in%
              unlist(input$domainShow),]
})

analytics

})
```

Note that when you use `invalidateLater()` you must put all other dependencies in `isolate()`, otherwise it will re-execute *both* when the time elapses or when the inputs change. Of course, this is another contrived example, it's highly unlikely your users really want to query the Analytics API every 10 seconds.

More advanced topics in Shiny

The remainder of this chapter will be spent looking at some of the other functions that Shiny includes that can give your users a smoother and more well-featured experience.

Finely controlling inputs and outputs

Shiny offers a variety of functions that allow you to directly control the user interface. You can program functions that take direct control over any of the input widgets, changing their labels, input range, or current selection, as well as switching the tabs on a tabsetPanel()-based UI, all using built-in functions. The following example uses updateCheckboxGroupInput(), which, as its name implies, is used to update the parameters of a checkboxGroupInput()-based widget. We also need the observe() function to make it work.

The observe() function is for reactive functions that do not return objects but rather are run for their effect—controlling parts of the user interface, creating files, and so on. In this example we are going to use it to control the UI, but don't forget that it can be used for lots of other purposes.

Let's see how they both work together to achieve the desired effect. In the basic version of the GA application we made things simple by assuming that if a user deselected both "NHS" and "Other" users, they wanted results from both returned. This is okay, but it's not very intuitive. It is far better to just take control of the UI and ensure that only valid inputs can be selected (perhaps adding some help text so users do not think the application is bugged). This is achieved very simply for this checkbox group as follows:

```
observe({

  if(class(input$domainShow) != "character"){

    updateCheckboxGroupInput(session, "domainShow",
                      choices = list("NHS users" = "NHS",
                                          "Other" = "Other"),
                      selected = "NHS users")

  }
})
```

Note that updateCheckboxGroupInput() also takes a session argument. Other than that extra detail, the updateCheckboxGroupInput() function is very simple to use and allows you to completely redraw the widget—so you could, in theory, add or take away options as well.

For our purposes, we just wish to check to see if the input is valid (invalid in this case means that both checkboxes are unchecked, which in turn means that input$domainShow does not return a valid character input), and if it is not, we tell the application to select the "NHS" checkbox.

A nice side effect of controlling the UI like this is that we now don't have to test elsewhere for valid inputs. So within the reactive function that returns `passData()` we can now omit the following:

```
if(class(input$domainShow)=="character"){
   ...
}
```

This is because we know the input is always valid because we wrote code that ensures that it is. Controlling user inputs so that they are always valid can be a useful way of writing clean and simple code, and letting your users know what is and isn't possible at the same time.

In the following example we will use `observe()` again for a more advanced purpose—controlling the user interface based on the URL which the user uses to access the server.

Reading client information and GET requests in Shiny

Shiny includes some very useful functionality that allows you to read information from a client's web browser, such as information from the URL (including GET search requests), size of plots in pixels, and so on.

All you need to do, as before, is run `shinyServer()` with a `session` argument. This causes, among other things, an object to be created that holds information about a client's session called `session$clientData`.

The exact content of this object will depend on what is open on the screen. The following objects will always exist:

```
url_hostname # hostname, e.g. localhost or chrisbeeley.net

url_pathname = # path, e.g. / or /shiny

url_port = # port number (8100 for localhost, can optionally
           # change when hosting, see chapter 5)

url_protocol = # highly likely to be http:

url_search = # the text after the "?" in the URL. In the following
           # example this will read "?person=NHS&smooth=yes".
```

Different output types will yield different information. Plots will give the following, among other return values:

```
output_myplot_height = # in pixels
output_myplot_width = # in pixels
```

There are many applications to which this information can be put, such as giving different UIs or default settings to users from different domains, or configuring graphs and other outputs based on their size (for example, for users who are using mobile devices or 32" monitors). We're going to look at perhaps the most obvious and powerful use of client data: the search string.

Custom interfaces from GET strings

In this example we're going to pretend that we have two groups of users who are going to want very different default reporting options. The NHS staff want to check the data before they start and are interested in the level of engagement the site generates. In order to do this, they want to start on the text summary tab and be given the bounce rate as default.

Members of the public are quite different. They know public money has been spent on the site and they want to see that there are plenty of visitors. They want to be taken straight to a graph summarizing the number of visitors over a date range.

We will also make the presence of a smoothing line preset so that we can give it by default for those who want it and exclude it for those who would be confused by it.

As well as the work with the GET query, the only extra bit we will need here is a function to change the selected panel from a tabsetPanel(). This is done, unsurprisingly, using the updateTabsetPanel() command.

Catering for these different needs is very easily done by creating URLs that encode the preferences and giving them to the different groups. To simplify the code, we will pretend that, if they are passed at all, the correct number of search terms are always passed in the correct order. This is a reasonable assumption if you write the URLs yourself. In a real-world example, the URLs are most likely going to be generated programmatically from a UI. Correctly parsing them is not too challenging, but it is not really the focus of the discussion here.

The following are the two URLs we will give out:

- `feedbacksite.nhs.uk/shiny?person=NHS&smooth=yes`
- `feedbacksite.nhs.uk/shiny?person=other&smooth=no`

As in the previous example, the code is wrapped in `observe()` and the first portion of the code returns the search terms from the URL as a named list:

```
observe({

  searchString <- parseQueryString(session$clientData$url_search)

  ...
```

Having done this we can then check that a `searchString` exists (in case other users land from the default URL) and, if it does, change the settings accordingly. The `updateTabsetPanel()` command uses a lot of the concepts we already saw when we read the tab that was selected. The function takes a `session` argument, an `inputId` argument (the name of the panel), and a `selected` argument (the name of the tab):

```
if(length(searchString)>0){ # if the searchString exists

  # deal with first query which indicates the audience
  if(searchString[[1]] == "nhs"){ #for NHS users do the following

    updateCheckboxGroupInput(session, "domainShow",
                          choices = list("NHS users" = "NHS",
                                              "Other" = "Other"),
                          selected = "NHS")

    updateRadioButtons(session, "outputType",
                      choices = list("Visitors" = "visitors",
                              "Bounce rate" = "bounceRate",
                              "Time on site" = "timeOnSite"),
                      selected= "Bounce rate")

      updateTabsetPanel(session, inputId = "theTabs",
                        selected = "summary")

  }
```

The rest of the code looks like the following:

```
if(searchString[[1]] == "other"){ # for the public do this
  ... # set up interface
  }
  # do they want a smooth?
  if(searchString[[2]] == "yes"){

    updateCheckboxInput(session, inputId = "smoother",
                        value = TRUE)

  }
```

This is clearly a very powerful way to make the experience better for your users completely transparently. You may wish to spend a bit of time setting up a web interface in whatever language you like (PHP, JavaScript, and so on) and correctly parsing the URLs that you generate within Shiny. If you need to handle varying lengths and names of lists, you will need a few extra commands:

- `names(theList)`: This will give you the name of each return value
- `length(unlist(theList))`: This will tell you how long the list is

Animation

Animation is surprisingly easy. The `sliderInput()` function that you have already seen, which is used to select the hours of interest within the application, has an optional animation function that will increment a variable by a set amount every time a specified unit of time elapses. This allows you to very easily produce a graphic that animates. In the following example we are going to look at the monthly graph and plot a linear trend line through the first 20% of the data (0 to 20% of the data). Then we are going to increment the percentage value that selects the portion of the data by 5% and plot a linear through that portion of data (5 to 25% of the data). Then increment again to 10 to 30% and plot another line, and so on. The following screenshot shows a static image of it:

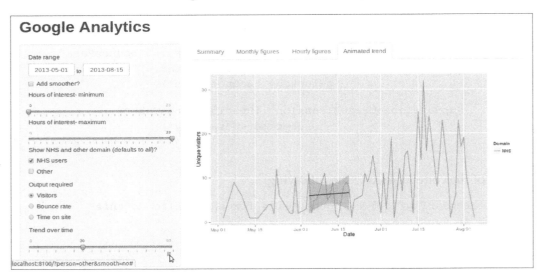

The GitHub page (`https://github.com/ChrisBeeley/GoogleAnalyticsAdvanced`) contains a link to a hosted version of the application so you can see for yourself.

The slider input is set up as follows, with an ID, label, minimum value, maximum value, initial value, step between values, and the animation options, giving the delay in milliseconds and whether the animation should loop:

```
sliderInput("animation", "Trend over time",
            min = 0, max = 80, value = 0, step = 5,
            animate=animationOptions(interval=1000, loop=FALSE))
```

Having set this up, the animated graph code is pretty simple, looking very much like the monthly graph data except with the linear smooth based on a subset of the data instead of the whole dataset. The graph is set up as before, and then a subset of the data is produced on which the linear smooth can be based:

```
smoothData <- graphData[graphData$Date %in%
            quantile(graphData$Date,
              input$animation/100, type=1):
            quantile(graphData$Date,
              (input$animation+20)/100, type=1),]
```

We won't get too distracted by this code, but essentially, it tests to see which of the whole date range falls in a range defined by percentage quantiles based on the `sliderInput()` values. See `?quantile` for more information.

Finally, the linear smooth is drawn with an extra data argument to tell ggplot2 to base the line only on the smaller `smoothData` object and not the whole range:

```
theGraph <- theGraph + geom_smooth(data = smoothData,
                                   method = "lm",
                                   colour = "black")
```

Not bad for a few lines of code. We have both ggplot2 and Shiny to thank for how easy this is.

Advanced graphics options

Although `renderPlot()` makes it very easy to produce reactive outputs, as we've seen, it only works with the standard method of outputting graphics in R. Images from certain packages within R, as well as images created outside of R, will not be displayed. Helpfully, Shiny includes a function to render all image files within a Shiny application: `renderImage()`. The simplest case is where you have a pre-rendered image that you wish to include. In the `server.R` file, the `renderImage()` call is made, returning a list with the path to the image and optionally the content type (to save Shiny from having to guess based on the file extension):

```
output$imageFile <- renderImage({
  list(src = "foo.png", contentType = "image/png")
}, deleteFile = FALSE)
```

The `deleteFile` argument is set to `false`; otherwise the file will be removed after display. This is intended for when the image is generated within the call. The file is no longer needed, so it can be deleted after the image is displayed.

Finally, the `ui.R` just includes the following:

```
imageOutput("imageFile")
```

Downloading graphics

The option to download graphics can be added easily using `downloadHandler()`. Essentially, `downloadHandler()` has two arguments that both contain functions—one to define the path to which the download should go, and one that defines what is to be downloaded. We'll go through the following code from `server.R` step-by-step:

```
output$downloadData.trend <- downloadHandler(

  filename <- function() {
    paste("Trend_plot", Sys.Date(),".png",sep="") },
```

This is the `filename()` function, and as you can see, it produces a filename `Trend_plot_XX_.png` where XX is the current date:

```
    content <- function(file) {
      png(file, width = 980, height = 400,
        units = "px", pointsize = 12,
        bg = "white", res = NA)

    trend.plot <- myTrend()

    print(trend.plot)

    dev.off()},
```

This is the `content()` function, and as you can see, it opens a png device (`?png`), calls a reactive function named `myTrend()`, which draws the graph, prints to the device, and then closes with a call to `dev.off()`. You can set up the `myTrend()` function very simply; in this case, it is just like the function that draws the graph itself except instead of being wrapped in `renderPlot()` to indicate that it is a Shiny output, it is just defined as a reactive function:

```
myTrend <- reactive({

    graphData <- ddply(passData(), .(Domain, Date), numcolwise(sum))
```

```
... rest of function as in the monthly graph function
```

```
})
```

Lastly the following is given to tell Shiny what type of file to expect:

```
contentType = 'image/png')
```

Note that having made `myTrend()` a reactive function, you can now use it in a standard `renderPlot()` call to draw it on the page like the following:

```
output$TrendPlot <- renderPlot({

  print(myTrend())

})
```

As you might have probably realized by now, in a real application, you wouldn't define the output twice; you would just write the function once, make it reactive, and then make use of that same function in the `renderPlot()` and `downloadHandler()` functions. As with many of the examples in this book, this code is designed to be easy to understand and is not realistic in terms of an actual application.

Adding the download button to the `ui.R` file is simple; the `downloadButton()` function takes the name of the download handler as defined in `server.R` and a label for the button:

```
tabPanel("Trend", plotOutput("TrendPlot"),
  downloadButton("downloadData.trend","Download Graph"))
```

As you can see, I have added the button underneath the graph so users know what they are downloading.

Downloading and uploading data

Downloading data is done in a very similar fashion, with the `downloadHandler()` call looking like the following:

```
output$downloadData <- downloadHandler(
filename = function(){
  "myData.csv"
}
content = function(file){
  write.csv(passData(), file)
}
)
```

Uploading data is achieved using the `fileInput()` function. In the following example, we will assume the user wishes to upload a comma-separated spreadsheet (`.csv`) file. The button is added to `ui.R` in the following manner:

```
fileInput("uploadFile", "Upload your own CSV file")
```

This button allows a user to select their own `.csv` file and makes a variety of objects based on the ID (in this case, `input$uploadFile$...`) available from `server.R`. The most useful is `input$uploadFile$datapath`, which is a path to the file itself and can be turned into a dataframe using `read.csv()`:

```
userData <- read.csv(input$uploadFile$datapath)
```

There are other bits of information about the file available; see `?fileInput` for more details.

Summary

Having finished this chapter, you have now seen most of the functionality within Shiny. It's a relatively small but powerful toolbox with which you can build a vast array of useful and intuitive applications with comparatively little effort. In this respect, ggplot2 is rather a good companion for Shiny because it too offers you a fairly limited selection of functions with which knowledgeable users can very quickly build many different graphical outputs.

In this chapter we have looked at fine-tuning the UI using `conditionalPanel()` and `observe()`, and changing your UI reactively. We also looked at managing slow computations using Shiny's reactivity functions, customizing a user's experience using client data, custom graphics and animation, and uploading and downloading data.

In the next chapter we will cover sharing your creations with the R community, which can be easily achieved using Shiny's built-in functions. We will also look at sharing your application with the whole world by hosting Shiny on a server. Both free DIY and paid options are discussed.

5
Running and Sharing Your Creations

Having made all of these wonderfully intuitive and powerful applications, you are quite naturally going to want to show them off. You may wish to share them with colleagues or members of the worldwide R community. You may wish to share them with individuals in your department or field who, while not R users, can handle a little bit of effort to get an application working. Or you may wish to share them transparently and freely with the whole world by hosting them on a server. Shiny offers quite a lot of approaches to sharing applications and you'll be glad to hear that even the most complex should not be too taxing with the right hardware and OS on your server. In this chapter we will look at the following:

- Sharing your work with R users using Gist/GitHub
- Using .zip and .tar files locally or over the Internet to share an application
- Sharing over the Web using free and paid-for hosting and technologies from RStudio
- Browser compatibility within Shiny

Sharing with the R community

Sharing with the R community is a little easier than with a general audience for two reasons:

- They can run the Shiny package within R and therefore use the Shiny functions designed to help distribute Shiny packages
- They are almost guaranteed to be reasonably knowledgeable about some of the processes that help you distribute an application, for example, unzipping directories

There are a few ways of sharing with R users running the Shiny package within R, as summarized in the following sections.

Sharing over GitHub

By far, the easiest way of sharing your creations with fellow R users is over GitHub (github.com). Of course, other R users can also use all the other methods in this chapter, but this is probably the most frictionless method (short of hosting the application) for both you and the end user.

Introduction to Git

You will no doubt have heard of Git (git-scm.com — the version control system that has collaborative sharing features at GitHub) even if you have never used it. Git is a version control system that can be used locally on your computer or, to get the best out of it, the version control repository on your computer can be synced online at GitHub. Hosting of open source code at GitHub is free, and there are paid options for closed source code. If you don't already use version control, this is an excellent reason to start. It is a little intimidating for newcomers, but over time, the resources and tutorials on the site have improved and perhaps one day of head scratching awaits you. Trust me, that one day will be paid back one hundredfold.

As a diehard Linux enthusiast, it pains me to admit it, but I actually found learning on Windows easier because they provide a wonderful GUI to get you started (also on OS X). This is not at all to say that you need to use Windows or should stick with Windows; I quite happily dropped the GUI and went to the terminal in Linux once I'd found my feet a bit. It's worth noting also that there are some great GUIs for Linux too, check your package management system. I didn't find any that supported beginners quite so well as the official Windows/ OS X versions, though.

Finally, and wonderfully, RStudio itself actually supports Git, and, once you've installed Git and set up your account, you can pretty much run the whole show from within RStudio itself. Just install Git, start an RStudio project within a directory and configure version control within the project options menu.

Sharing applications using Git

Do consult the websites given previously for more details about each of these steps. Once you've set your Git version control, and paired with an online repository at GitHub, you can very easily share your creations with anyone running the R and Shiny package by using the runGitHub() command, which takes as mandatory arguments the name of the repository and the username.

For example, to run the Google Analytics application from *Chapter 2, Building Your First Application*, just run the following line of code:

```
runGitHub("GoogleAnalytics", "ChrisBeeley")
```

Code and data are both automatically downloaded and run, and with the default argument (`launch.browser = TRUE`) used, a browser is launched to view the application.

If you don't want or need version control and don't need data to be included in the download, a simpler option is to use Gist, which is also hosted at GitHub at `gist.github.com`.

Using Gist is simply a matter of visiting the URL, setting up an account, pasting your code in, and giving the `server.R` and `ui.R` files the correct filenames. You will then have a URL with which to show others your code. Running this code from the Shiny package is just a matter of using `runGist()` with the URL or even just the unique numeric identifier from the URL:

```
runGist("https://gist.github.com/ChrisBeeley/6272654")
runGist("6272654")
runGist(6272654)
```

These are all valid methods of running the minimal example from *Chapter 2, Building Your First Application*.

Sharing using .zip and .tar

Probably the next most frictionless method of distributing a Shiny application to R users is by hosting either a `.zip` or `.tar` file of your application either over the Web or FTP. You will need somewhere to host the file, and then users can run the application simply using `runUrl()` in the following manner:

```
runUrl("http://www.myserver/shinyapps/myshinyapp.zip")
```

Note that this URL is not real; replace it with the address to your own file.

Of course, you can distribute a `.zip` file any way you like—your users only need to unzip and then use `runApp()` from within the directory just as you do when testing the application. You could e-mail the file, distribute on a USB drive—any method you choose. The disadvantages to this method are, firstly, your users have to unzip the file themselves (although this is unlikely to confuse many R users) and, secondly, any changes to the application will also need to be distributed manually.

Sharing with the world

In most cases, any serious work you do with Shiny will at some point need to be shared with a non-R user, whether it's a non-technical colleague in your department or the whole of the Internet. In this case, a bit more of the legwork falls onto you, but you should still be pleasantly surprised how simple the process is. There are two options here: set up your own server or get a paid account with RStudio to do it for you.

Glimmer

Glimmer is the name of the server on which RStudio will host your applications for you (a second server, Spark, has recently been added). At the time of writing, this service is in beta and is therefore free; there are plans to make it into a paid service although these are as yet unconfirmed. The only drawbacks at present are that you may not wish to copy your code and/or data to a third party and you cannot exercise any control over server uptime, responsiveness, and so on. If in the future it becomes paid, you will presumably have more guarantees over things such as server uptime and latency, but of course you will have to pay for it.

Shiny Server

If you don't want to pay and/or don't want to copy your data to RStudio's server, you can download and install **Shiny Server** (for Linux only) and do it yourself. Shiny Server is totally free and open source, which is a great credit to RStudio. They have a paid enterprise edition in the pipeline which will include a variety of useful things such as user authentication and launching multiple R processes for each user, but the free version is, in my experience, stable and well featured. Installation details can be found at `https://github.com/rstudio/shiny-server`.

Installation on Ubuntu is embarrassingly easy; even with my limited knowledge of running Linux servers, I had it up and running on my personal server in less than an hour. It's run quite happily ever since. Mileage with other distributions will vary, although judging from forum and blog posts, people have successfully run it on quite a variety of distributions. Depending on what you are doing with your application, one thing to be careful of is directory ownership and permissions. For example, one of my applications produces PDF files for download. This requires making Shiny the owner of the directory within the application folder which houses the temporary files that are produced for download, and making the directory writeable. Within a corporate environment, you may also find that the port Shiny uses is blocked by the firewall — changing to a different port is simply a matter of editing the configuration file as detailed on the Shiny Server webpage given previously.

Browser compatibility

The last thing that you will need to worry about when sharing your creations with the world is browser compatibility. On the whole, it's reasonable to assume that most home users are running Internet Explorer (IE) 9 (or 10) or another reasonably well-featured and up-to-date browser. However, corporate environments can be quite different and, even today, they are notorious for using old versions of Internet Explorer. Clearly, the best solution is to use an up-to-date browser in your organization, but if this is not possible, it's worth knowing the following.

When you launch a browser locally from your R session, for example, when you are writing your application, or running someone else's application with the methods in the earlier part of this chapter, only Internet Explorer 10 is supported. However, when running over Shiny Server, Explorer 8 and 9 are both supported. In my organization, the web developers with whom we worked even had success running over IE7 using various compatibility tweaks; however, this is not simple and is outside the scope of this chapter.

Summary

In this chapter we have learned several methods for sharing your Shiny applications with the world. This process is very easy indeed with fellow users of R, and a little harder with the whole Internet, but however you do it I'm sure you'll agree that it was relatively painless and worth the effort. In this chapter we have discussed beginning to use Git and GitHub (and Gist) and using them to share your code and applications with other R users. We also looked at distributing Shiny applications manually or over FTP to R users using `.zip` and `.tar` files. We covered hosting solutions to share your application with the whole Internet, including Glimmer and Shiny Server and future directions for each. Lastly, we discussed compatibility issues that Shiny has with old versions of Internet Explorer, and when you do, and don't need to worry about them.

Index

Symbols

A

B

C

D

E

Eclipse 8
elements
  displaying, of user interface 64
  hiding, of user interface 64
Emacs 8
Emacs Speaks Statistics plugin 8
examples
  running, within Shiny 17-19

F

fileInput() function 82
functions 13

G

GET requests
  reading, in Shiny 75
ggplot2 14
Git
  about 84
  used, for sharing applications 84, 85
GitHub
  creations, sharing over 84
  URL 84
Glimmer 86
Google Analytics 41
Google Analytics application
  about 28
  code 38
  data processing 32
  optional exercise 38
  outputs 35-38
  reactive objects 33, 34
  UI 28-31
graphics
  downloading 80, 81
grep() command 46

H

headerPanel() 23
HTML
  used, for customizing Shiny applications 42

HTML() function 43
htmlOutput() function 43

I

indexing 11
input$comment 26
inputId argument 23
inputs
  controlling, with isolate() function 70-72
installation, R 6
installation, Shiny 17
interface
  controlling, with submitButton()
       function 70
invalidateLater() command 72, 73
invalidateLater() function 69
isolate() function 69, 70
  used, for controlling specific inputs 70-72

J

JavaScript
  Shiny applications, customizing 52
jQuery 56

L

label argument 23
length() command 38
line charts 15
lists 11

M

mainPanel() function 23
matrices 12
minimal HTML interface
  about 47
  index.html file 48-50
  server.R file 50, 51

N

names
  providing, to tabPanel elements 64-67
NHS 29
Notepad ++ with the NppToR plugin 7

O

objects 13
observe() function 74

P

passData object 33
paste() method 38
Patient Opinion
  about 42
  URL 42
plot() function 13
png 51
poly() command 51
print() method 36

R

R
  about 5, 6
  arrays 12
  code editors 7
  dataframes 10, 11
  data, loading 9, 10
  functions 13
  ggplot2 14
  help, obtaining 8, 9
  IDEs 7
  learning 8
  lists 11
  matrices 12
  objects 13
  variable types 12
radioButtons() method 31
R community
  applications, sharing with 83
R console 6, 7
reactive functions
  running, over time 72, 73
  using, effectively 69
reactive object
  about 33, 34
  using, effectively 69
reactive programming paradigm 17

reactive user interfaces
  about 67
  server.R example 68
  ui.R example 68
renderImage() function 79
renderPlot() function 79
renderText() 26
rga package 28
RKWard 7, 17
RStudio 8, 17, 84
runApp() method 23, 85
runGist() method 85
runGitHub() command 84
runUrl() method 85

S

server.R
  of minimal example 24, 25
server.R file 68
Shiny
  about 42
  advanced topics 73
  browser compatibility 87
  custom HTML links 42
  installing 17
  URL, for tutorial pages 68
Shiny applications
  customizing, HTML used 42
  customizing, JavaScript used 52
  customizing, jQuery used 56
  running 41
Shiny applications, with JavaScript
  server.R file 54, 55
  ui.R file 52
Shiny applications, with jQuery
  about 56
  index.html file 56, 57
  jQuery code 58-60
  server.R file 57, 58
Shiny package 5
Shiny program
  running, on local machine 22, 23
Shiny Server 86
sidebarPanel() function 23, 64

sliderInput() function 30, 78
Spark 86
StatET plugin 8
submitButton() function 69, 70
  used, for controlling interface 70
switch() command 47

T

table() command 14
tabPanel elements
  names, providing to 64-67
tar file
  used, for sharing applications 85
textInput() 23
Tinn-R 8

U

UI 28, 29
ui.R
  of minimal example 22
ui.R file 68
updateCheckboxGroupInput() function 74

updateTabsetPanel() command 76
user interface
  elements, displaying 64
  elements, hiding 64

V

value argument 23
variables
  extracting, from dataframes 10
variable types 12
Vim 8
Vim-R plugin 8

W

widget
  types 26, 27

Z

zip file
  used, for sharing applications 85

Thank you for buying
Web Application Development with R Using Shiny

About Packt Publishing

Packt, pronounced 'packed', published its first book "*Mastering phpMyAdmin for Effective MySQL Management*" in April 2004 and subsequently continued to specialize in publishing highly focused books on specific technologies and solutions.

Our books and publications share the experiences of your fellow IT professionals in adapting and customizing today's systems, applications, and frameworks. Our solution based books give you the knowledge and power to customize the software and technologies you're using to get the job done. Packt books are more specific and less general than the IT books you have seen in the past. Our unique business model allows us to bring you more focused information, giving you more of what you need to know, and less of what you don't.

Packt is a modern, yet unique publishing company, which focuses on producing quality, cutting-edge books for communities of developers, administrators, and newbies alike. For more information, please visit our website: www.packtpub.com.

About Packt Open Source

In 2010, Packt launched two new brands, Packt Open Source and Packt Enterprise, in order to continue its focus on specialization. This book is part of the Packt Open Source brand, home to books published on software built around Open Source licences, and offering information to anybody from advanced developers to budding web designers. The Open Source brand also runs Packt's Open Source Royalty Scheme, by which Packt gives a royalty to each Open Source project about whose software a book is sold.

Writing for Packt

We welcome all inquiries from people who are interested in authoring. Book proposals should be sent to author@packtpub.com. If your book idea is still at an early stage and you would like to discuss it first before writing a formal book proposal, contact us; one of our commissioning editors will get in touch with you.

We're not just looking for published authors; if you have strong technical skills but no writing experience, our experienced editors can help you develop a writing career, or simply get some additional reward for your expertise.

Mastering Web Application Development with AngularJS

ISBN: 978-1-78216-182-0   Paperback: 372 pages

Build single-page web applications using the power of AngularJS

1. Make the most out of AngularJS by understanding the AngularJS philosophy and applying it to real life development tasks

2. Effectively structure, write, test, and finally deploy your application

3. Add security and optimization features to your AngularJS applications

4. Harness the full power of AngularJS by creating your own directives

Express Web Application Development

ISBN: 978-1-84969-654-8   Paperback: 236 pages

Learn how to develop web applications with the Express framework from scratch

1. Exploring all aspects of web development using the Express framework

2. Starts with the essentials

3. Expert tips and advice covering all Express topics

Please check **www.PacktPub.com** for information on our titles

Learning RStudio for R Statistical Computing

ISBN: 978-1-78216-060-1   Paperback: 126 pages

Learn to effectively perform R development, statistical analysis, and reporting with the most popular RIDE

1. A complete practical tutorial for RStudio, designed keeping in mind the needs of analysts and R developers alike

2. Step-by-step examples that apply the principles of reproducible research and good programming practices to R projects

3. Learn to effectively generate reports, create graphics, and perform analysis, and even build R-packages with RStudio

Web Application Development with Yii and PHP

ISBN: 978-1-84951-872-7   Paperback: 332 pages

Lean the Yii application development framework by taking a step-by-step approch to building a Web-based project tast tracking system from conception through production depolyment

1. A step-by-step guide to creating a modern Web application using PHP, MySQL, and Yii

2. Build a real-world, user-based, database-driven project task management application using the Yii development framework

3. Start with a general idea, and finish with deploying to production, learning everything about Yii inbetween, from "A"ctive record to "Z"ii component library

Please check **www.PacktPub.com** for information on our titles